Using

TAKING↻SIDES

in the Classroom

**Contemporary
Learning Series**

2460 Kerper Blvd., Dubuque, IA 52001

Visit us on the Internet
http://www.mhcls.com/usingts/usingts.pdf

Credits

"Psychology and Contemporary Issues" course syllabus and outline prepared by Dr. Michael Reiner, associate professor of psychology, Kennesaw State College, Marietta, GA. Reprinted by permission.

"Debating the Issues: Adopting Critical Thinking in Contemporary Marketing Curricula" section on dialectical thinking by Bart Macchiette. Reprinted by permission.

"Scored Discussions," by John Zola, *Social Education* (October 1989) p. 370. Reprinted by permission of the National Council for the Social Studies and the author.

"Leading Class Discussions of Controversial Issues," by Thomas E. Kelly, *Social Education* (October 1989), pp. 368–370. Reprinted by permission of the National Council for the Social Studies and the author.

"Debate Evaluation Form" and "Debate Sign-up Sheet," prepared by Professor Neil Sapper, who teaches History of the United States in the Department of Social Sciences, Amarillo College, Amarillo, TX. Reprinted by permission.

"I'll Take My Stand," an issue evaluation form prepared by Professor James Kilbride, who teaches in the Department of Psychology and Education, Miami-Dade Community College, Miami, FL. Reprinted by permission.

Spark a debate in your classroom!

Taking Sides

The **Taking Sides** volumes present current issues in a debate-style format designed to stimulate student interest and develop critical thinking skills. Each issue is thoughtfully framed with an issue summary, an issue introduction, and a postscript. The pro and con essays—selected for their liveliness and substance—represent the arguments of leading scholars and commentators in their fields. **Taking Sides** readers feature annotated listings of selected World Wide Web sites. An instructor's resource guide with testing material is available for each volume.

www.mhcls.com/takingsides

Preface

The Taking Sides series is a very successful tool for exposing college and university students to the controversies in their discipline of study and for reinforcing their critical thinking skills. The program began in 1978 with *Taking Sides: Clashing Views on Controversial Political Issues,* now called simply *Political Issues.* Since then, thousands of instructors around the world have incorporated these volumes into a wide range of instructional programs. We currently have more than 50 Taking Sides volumes in numerous areas of study. For a list of current Taking Sides volumes, go to: *http://www.mhcls.com/online/contentsmain.mhtml.*

Over the years, instructors have developed a number of techniques to engage students in a pro/con examination of important issues, techniques for use in large lecture classes at the introductory level as well as for more advanced, seminar-type courses. The common element in these techniques is a belief in the value of teaching with a dialectic approach, coupled with the recognition that controversies do exist—controversies concerning many of the most pressing issues across disciplines.

This guide represents a sample of the techniques designed for teaching with a debate format. Many of these techniques have been developed by users of Taking Sides. We include several student handouts and appendices to help you translate these techniques to your course requirements. *Using Taking Sides in the Classroom* is not intended to be a comprehensive reflection of the full range of instructional methods that have arisen as a result of classroom use of Taking Sides; rather, it is meant to demonstrate the flexibility of the individual Taking Sides volumes and to show that any classroom setting can easily be adapted to allow for the exploration of controversial issues.

Instructors committed to the development of critical thinking skills have discovered that a Taking Sides volume is a good tool to do so, and we are passing along some of their insights about this approach. To quote from Professor Michael Reiner, whose course outline for using *Taking Sides: Clashing Views on Controversial Psychological Issues* is reproduced in **Appendix 1:**

> Numerous reports on improving higher education have emphasized the need to encourage students to engage in active learning and critical thinking (e.g., *Seven Principles of Good Practice in Undergraduate Education,* American Association for Higher Education). To accomplish these goals, faculty often must abandon well-established teaching practices, such as the lecture, and adopt more innovative pedagogical methods . . . [W]e know that students often learn best when actively engaged in the learning process .... [E]ncouraging critical thought, not just rote memorization, actively engages the students' higher-order thinking skills, thereby facilitating comprehension, analysis, and synthesis. (from remarks delivered at the Southeast Psychological Association Meeting, Spring 1995)

This edition of *Using Taking Sides in the Classroom* reflects the efforts of a number of dedicated educators who have created methods for using Taking Sides in their classes. We wish to acknowledge their contributions, especially the following: Kurt Finsterbusch, Department of Sociology, University of Maryland; Dan Gallagher, Department of Psychology, Salisbury State College; James M. Kilbride, Department of Psychology and Education, Miami-Dade Community College South; Larry Madaras, Department of History, Howard Community College; George McKenna, Department of Political Science, City College, CUNY; Michael Reiner, Department of Psychology, Kennesaw State College; Brent Slife, Department of Psychology, Brigham Young University; and Thomas R. Swartz, Department of Economics, University of Notre Dame.

Individual instructor's manuals are prepared for each of the Taking Sides volumes. Each manual consists of instructional aid that corresponds to each issue in the volume, including a synopsis of each author's position on the issues, teaching and discussion suggestions, and multiple-choice, and essay questions. Copies of these manuals can be obtained by contacting our faculty support center through The McGraw-Hill Companies at: 800–338–3787 (Hightstown, NJ) or 800–565–5758 (Canada).

Lastly, we invite you to visit our Website for the Taking Sides series at *http://www.mhcls.com/ online/contentsmain.mhtml*. We value your involvement in the program. If you have teaching techniques you would like to share, improvements you would like to see to a Taking Sides volume, or ideas for new areas in which you would like to see a title, please use the contact information below. For your convenience, we have a *We Want Your Advice* form on page 48 that can be filled out and returned to us as a prepaid business reply envelope. Or, visit our Web site to submit your feedback electronically: http://tilde.mhedu.com/tsAdboardForm.mhtml. Together we can build a teaching tool that will allow you, the instructor, to give the most of yourself to your students.

The Taking Sides program is always looking for academic advisory board members to offer opinions on developing texts. If you would like to become a member of the Taking Sides academic advisory board, or if you have an idea for a new title, use the contact information below. We will use your insights to develop the kind of thought-provoking titles that will enliven your class through the study of controversial issues.

Larry Loeppke
Managing Editor
McGraw-Hill Contemporary Learning Series
larry_loeppke@mcgraw-hill.com

Contents

PART 3: APPENDICES 39

PART 1

Background and Basics

CHAPTER 1

The Taking Sides Series

Welcome to the Taking Sides series. Each volume in this series is designed to provide readers with well-developed, carefully considered, and sharply opposed positions on a wide range of issues. The purpose of the debate format is to stimulate interest in the subject matter and to encourage critical thinking. The pro and con essays reflect a variety of ideological positions and have been selected by the Taking Sides authors for their liveliness and because of their value in a debate framework. The selections are written by scholars and commentators who are respected and accomplished in their fields.

Each issue in each of the volumes in the Taking Sides series has an issue introduction, which sets the stage for the debate, provides some background information on each author, and generally puts the issue into context. Each issue concludes with a postscript that briefly summarizes the debate, gives the reader paths for further investigation, and suggests additional readings that might be helpful. Each volume in the Taking Sides series concludes with a list of contributors (with a brief biography of each contributor) and an index.

Understanding the complexity of our society requires thought and a sensitivity to the continuum of views of all important issues. The volumes of the Taking Sides series provide a starting point for fostering critical thinking and serious dialogue. Each volume has been designed to accomplish the following:

- Provide students with well-developed, carefully considered, and sharply opposed points of view on enduring issues in a field of study.

- Help students to understand the significance of the principles, concepts, and theories they are learning in class by demonstrating their relevance to vital issues that they will confront throughout their lives.

- Encourage students to apply critical thinking techniques to the opinions and statements that they see and hear around them.

- Promote the personal resolution of important issues by challenging assumptions and unconscious biases.

- Stimulate students to synthesize their own positions by clarifying and understanding values.

- Develop students' understanding and appreciation for the nature and value of evidence in forming an opinion.

Current Taking Sides Titles

The volumes currently available in the Taking Sides Series are listed below. The links are available at the following URL: http://www.mhcls.com/takingsides/ts-list.mhtml. To find more information about each volume as well as its table of contents, click on the title you wish to review

- 2005 Taking Sides Set, 3/e
- 20th Century American History, 1/e
- Abnormal Psychology, 2/e
- African Issues, 1/e
- American Foreign Policy
- American History, Volume 1, 12/e
- American History, Volume 2, 12/e
- Anthropology
- Bioethical Issues
- Business Ethics and Society
- Childhood and Society
- Classroom Management, 1/e
- Cognitive Science, 1/e
- Crime and Criminology, 6/e
- Criminal Justice, 1/e
- Cultural Anthropology, 1/e
- Drugs and Society, 6/e
- Early Childhood Education, 1/e
- Economic Issues, 11/e
- Educational Issues, 13/e
- Educational Psychology, 2/e
- Environmental Issues, 12/e
- Family and Personal Relationships, 6/e
- Food and Nutrition, 1/e
- Gender, 3/e
- Global Issues, 2/e
- Health and Society, 6/e
- Human Sexuality, 8/e
- Latin American Issues, 1/e
- Legal Issues, 10/e
- Lifespan Development, 1/e
- Management, 1/e
- Mass Media and Society, 7/e
- Moral Issues, 10/e
- Physical Anthropology, 1/e
- Political Issues, 13th Edition (Rev. Ed.), 13/e
- Psychological Issues, 12/e
- Public Policy, Justice, and the Law, 1/e
- Race and Ethnicity, 5/e
- Religion, 1/e

- Science, Technology, and Society, 6/e
- Social Issues, 11/e
- Social Psychology, 1/e
- Special Education, 1/e
- Teaching and Educational Practice, 2/e
- Western Civilization, 1/e
- World Civilizations, 2/e
- World History, Volume 1, 3/e
- World History, Volume 2, 2/e
- World Politics (Revised), 11/e

Controversy in the Classroom

Educators have always understood the importance of presenting conflicts of opinion in the learning process. Studies have given experimental support to the commonsense notion that students retain information better when they are actively engaged in the dialectical process. One study tested short and long-term recall on the basis of four different methods of organizing information: *dialectical, causative, problematic,* and *serial.* Of these, the dialectical method was shown to result in the highest rate of retention. Another study yielded similar results. Professor Brent Slife, Brigham Young University, prepared an abstract summary of these studies for this guide:

Two notable studies compared the effectiveness of various organizations of ideas (or "top-level structures") in facilitating learning. The first study, conducted by Meyer and Freedle (1979), organized the same set of ideas into four top-level structures commonly used in writing: dialectical—the ideas were organized in an opposing points-of-view framework; causative—the ideas were structured in a cause/effect format; problematic—the ideas were organized in a problem/solution structure; and serial—the ideas were ordered by listing them one by one. These four passages had an equal number of words, identical information (or ideas), and the same lower-level structure (as ensured by a prose analysis procedure). However, significantly more ideas and information were learned from the dialectically organized passage than from any other top-level structure, both in short-term and long-term recall.

The second study, conducted by Rickards and Slife (1982), replicated these results with college students and showed that the students who processed the information "deeply" or semantically (i.e., students low in dogmatism) profited the most from the dialectical organization. Highly dogmatic students normally attend to the surface quality of information and hence rarely use any top-level structures to their advantage. However, there was evidence that even these students began to see the implications and relations of the ideas better when the ideas were presented dialectically.

These findings clearly bear out the importance of dialectical organization in the presentation of information. Unfortunately, most texts assume one of the other top-level structures in their presentation of ideas. Many authors undoubtedly prefer certain top-level structures for certain types of information (such as "problem/solution" for empirical findings). Instructors seem to be caught between the structure preferences of text authors and the optimal text structure for learning.

The Taking Sides series, a line of supplemental-type books, may exemplify a solution to this dilemma. These books of readings cover many disciplines and have the characteristics of dialectical organization (i.e., pro and con articles on issues of the discipline). Using such a book as a supplement to the regular text may offer the benefits of a dialectical top-level structure, but it will not compromise the integrity of the information.

The results of these studies will not surprise veteran educators. At one time or another, most instructors have searched out and presented to their students views that are contrary to those presented in the standard course texts or in their own lectures. They are operating on the principle that truth can best be determined by the study of opposing viewpoints. However, in many instances it is difficult to transform this principle into a workable, systematic educational plan. If done randomly, the introduction of contradictory points of view may be confusing and may lead to frustration for both students and instructors. Yet it is very important for today's students to understand that experts can disagree and that for some questions there are no clear-cut answers.

The Taking Sides program was initiated to create a clearly directed, systematic approach to the study of controversial issues. Each Taking Sides volume presents the most coherent statements available on both sides of a multitude of current issues. In each of the many disciplines covered by Taking Sides volumes, an author has searched the literature to determine the most critical issues in that particular field. Care is taken to ensure that the issues presented can be easily integrated into introductory-level classes as well as into more advanced seminar situations.

Each issue within the Taking Sides volumes is self-contained and may be assigned according to the individual instructor's preferences or the dictates of classroom time. The introductions and postscripts that accompany each issue are written by the authors to provide the necessary background for an informed reading of the issue. The introductions reduce the need for background lectures and should increase the time available for discussion of critical information.

It is this final step of evaluation that often makes the essential difference between considered thought and passive recall. This belief is shared by each of the authors of the Taking Sides volumes as well. As Brent Slife writes in the volume introduction to *Taking Sides: Psychological Issues:*

Knowing the "facts" often is not enough to make useful decisions. It is seeing relationships after examining evidence from all sides and the development of personal insights that makes it worthwhile to gather "facts."

Practical Applications

While few would argue with this call for "eloquent expression of opposing views," there are other factors to consider when choosing a pedagogical approach. In most disciplines, introductory classes are large; because of this, instructors often believe that the discussion of multiple points of view can cause confusion and consume too much valuable course time. The Taking Sides series is designed to free instructors to inject as much or as little controversy into their classes as they believe can be handled comfortably. For instance, there are a number of ways you might approach the use of Taking Sides as a student reader:

- You might simply assign students to read particular issues at the time you cover the topic in class. (This method is used in the introductory economics program at the University of Notre Dame and in many other large lecture classes.)
- You might choose to have your students write summary papers of entire issues or selections within issues, showing how they amplify topics covered in class or in the text. (This has been done at Arizona State University in large introductory psychology classes.)
- If you choose to give test or quiz items on an assigned issue, you will find the instructor's manual that accompanies each volume to be quite helpful. Each manual contains test items in addition to a synopsis of each issue and guidelines for discussing the issue in class, if such discussion seems appropriate to you.
- You might have students give short oral reports to the class on a particular selection. This can lead to some of the other, more formal approaches to using Taking Sides in the classroom, such as debates and discussions. (These approaches are discussed in greater detail later.)
- If you supplement a textbook with Taking Sides, you may ask your students to correlate the issues in the Taking Sides book with the appropriate sections of the text.
- Students could be asked to do follow-up research and to find or develop alternative views on a particular issue.
- A simple approach (designed at Northern Virginia Community College) is to ask students to create and answer their own issue questions. The grades are based more on the validity of the questions than on the answers. This method is not time-consuming, and it tests students' grasp of the essential ideas being debated.

These and other methods are discussed here to allow for a smooth and ordered transition into the treatment of controversial issues in any classroom setting. Time is always in short supply, and you, as the instructor, will give more or less weight to particular issues according to the focus of the course. This need not prevent the addition of this material to your syllabus. The Taking Sides volumes have proven very successful in many different disciplines at all levels of intensity, from more content-oriented introductory settings to more theoretical upper-level seminars.

Criteria for Issue Selection. A guiding principle in the selection of the issues for all Taking Sides volumes, as well as the corresponding articles, is that they be easily understood and relevant to the backgrounds and interests of the students. Through our editorial and revision processes, we eliminate issues that prove to be uninteresting or not easily understood by the students. We actively solicit reactions from instructors for this purpose.

The issues that are selected are chosen for their broad applicability. Even students simply fulfilling a requirement in a discipline to which they may have no further exposure will have formed opinions on many of these issues. One of the important functions of the Taking Sides volumes is to force students as well as instructors to examine their opinions and beliefs in light of contradictory facts and evidence.

Evaluation. In addition to the concern for maintaining an ordered system in the classroom, there is the problem of evaluation. If an instructor ascribes strongly to a particular point of view, how can he or she objectively evaluate the learning and teaching processes? Subjectivity is an issue that has long plagued educators. How can we guard against hidden biases on the part of the instructor and a desire to please on the part of the student?

In this guide, we provide a variety of evaluation techniques and materials. Some are simple report forms to be filled in by the students and returned to the instructor or a teaching assistant. Others are more complex and are for use in evaluating the contribution and performance of members of the class during formal debate sessions. These include role-playing suggestions, numerical ratings for coherence of thought and presentation, and evaluation forms for use by the instructor and class members. These methods can allow for a more objective appraisal of issues for which there are—in the end—no right or wrong answers, only considered opinions.

Opinions, Conflict, and Truth. All of the evaluation methods presented in this guide are based on the value of studying conflicting opinion in order to establish the truth. Writers from Georg Hegel to Thomas Jefferson have recognized the importance of a struggle of ideas and warned against the danger of a monopoly by any one set of ideas.

The dialogue approach to education that is embodied in this guide and in the Taking Sides series embraces a philosophy as well as a pedagogical technique. With the aid of this guide, and through shared experiences with other instructors, any class can be enlivened through the study of controversial issues. The importance of this to the search for truth cannot be doubted. As John Milton wrote in *Aeropagitica*:

Though all the winds of doctrine were let loose to play upon the earth, so Truth be in the field, we do injuriously, by licensing the prohibiting, to misdoubt her strength. Let her and falsehood grapple; who ever knew Truth put to the worse, in a free and open encounter?

CHAPTER 2

Approaching the Classroom with Taking Sides

In this chapter, we present some of the classroom situations that can benefit with a Taking Sides volume and the approaches that instructors have used to incorporate Taking Sides into these situations. As a critical-thinking tool, a Taking Sides volume is particularly suited to:

1. reinforcing students critical thinking skills,
2. pulling students into classroom discussions, and
3. preparing for a class debate.

It is hoped that the techniques that we introduce will help you and your students get the most out of the Taking Sides reader. Some of the classroom techniques provided require greater attention on the instructor's part, while others demand that students pursue the additional information on their own. You may choose to combine two or more of the techniques to produce a detailed course outline, or you may prefer to use a single technique throughout the course (see **Appendix 1** for a sample course outline utilizing Taking Sides).

Teaching Students to Think Critically

The push is on for educators to help students strengthen their critical thinking skills. With the advent of new communication technologies, students are being exposed more frequently to differing viewpoints and sometimes questionable information. In order to process this information effectively, students are going to have to rely on their critical thinking skills. State governments, such as New Jersey, South Carolina, and Pennsylvania, are stressing the importance of teaching critical thinking skills, at the elementary and high school education levels.

What is critical thinking? Richard Paul, founder and director of Sonoma State University's Center for Critical Thinking, defines critical thinking as "[T]hinking about your thinking while you're thinking in order to make your thinking better. . . . To think well is to impose discipline and restraint on our thinking—by means of intellectual standards—in order to raise our thinking to a level of "perfection" or quality that is not natural or likely in undisciplined, spontaneous thought." (from an interview for *Think* magazine, April 1992). The Center for Critical Thinking maintains a Website at Sonoma State University with some instructional syllabi and information for the elementary and college level to help educators implement critical thinking in their teaching. You can visit the site at **http://www.criticalthinking.org/**. Several other Websites

have tutorials and syllabi for teaching and learning about critical thinking: **http://philosophy.hku.hk/think/** offers tutorials on reasoning, creativity, argument, analysis. **http://www.epistemelinks.com/Main/Topics.aspx?TopiCode=Reas** offers links to sites with puzzles, logical thinking exercises, paradoxes, logical fallacies. A search of critical thinking Websites will provide you with many sites relevant to your subject matter.

Taking Sides anthologies are an excellent tool for teaching critical thinking in that they expose students strongly argued opposing positions related to their field of study.

Critical Thinking Techniques

We have prepared a list of critical thinking questions, originally found at a Website for Salisbury State University, which easily translate to any discipline or course. They can help students better prepare to assess arguments and evidence as they write papers, prepare oral reports, or critically analyze positions taken by their classmates in a debate. You can find a student handout of these questions, called *Questions to Ask When Examining a Position*, on page 18. Although a brief explanation of each question is given in the handout, you may wish to discuss these questions with your students in class.

Questions to Ask When Examining a Position touches on a number of important topics to the teaching of critical thinking, including writer bias, propaganda, and reader bias. To alert students of writer bias, the American government program at Howard Community College in Maryland gives students bibliographic information on some of the most common sources for the material that they will encounter. These sources are also identified according to the editorial attitudes they reflect. This kind of information gives the student an indication as to the likely bias of the author. A guide such as this can be created for any discipline and distributed to students as a reference in their reading. An example is shown in Appendix 2.

We have created a *Propaganda Alert* student handout, which can be found on page 20 based on a 1997 edition of *Analyzing Controversy: An Introductory Guide* by Gary K. Clabaugh, La Salle University, and Edward G. Rozycki, Widener University. This handout introduces students to a number of propaganda techniques employed by writers, including generalizations, name calling, appeals to emotion, slogans, and presuppositions as one method of helping students become aware of their own biases when analyzing arguments. One way to reduce a possible "sympathetic effect" when considering an argument is to test students on their opinions of the issues before they are discussed.

Organized Methods for Evaluating Critical Thinking

Once students have been exposed to the processes of critical thinking, there are several ways in which their understanding of these techniques can be evaluated.

Understanding of these critical thinking methods would most clearly be demonstrated in a formal debate setting in which students apply critical thinking skills in an open and spontaneous setting. Under these conditions, an instructor can quickly and easily identify those students who show a clear grasp of the skills involved and those who do not demonstrate such an understanding.

In classroom situations where preparing formal debate is either impractical or undesirable, there are less formal methods for determining how much students have learned about critical thinking skills. A simple and straightforward device was developed specifically for Taking Sides by George McKenna at City College, City University of New York. A student handout for this issue report, called *Taking Sides Issue Report,* can be found on page 23. The questions in the handout demand an understanding of the skills and techniques that are required to analyze an argument. This method has the advantage of requiring the students to go to the library in order to conduct further research.

A more elaborate questionnaire was created at Diablo Valley Community College for use in a course entitled "Critical Reasoning in History." Much of the information that is solicited is similar to George McKenna's *Taking Sides Issue Report,* but much more detail is required. A student handout of this questionnaire, called *Taking Sides Analysis Report (Long Form),* can be found on page 24. It can be copied and given to students as a quiz or exam, or it can used as a guide to assist students as they read the issues in Taking Sides. Professor Dan Gallagher, Department of Psychology, Salisbury State University, prepared a similar short-form analysis questionnaire, called *Taking Sides Analysis Report (Short Form),* which is presented on page 26.

When teaching students critical thinking skills, you may find that the first assignment is difficult for students but that it becomes easier both for them to do and for you to grade as more are given. Once these techniques are firmly established and your students are comfortable with them, you can create a unified set of learning objectives. These objectives can be adapted quickly and easily for any issue area. Broad objectives can be derived from the essay questions contained in the instructor's manual that accompanies each volume, or they can be keyed to the development of particular skills or knowledge.

Having taught students analytical skills and distributed content-oriented material, it is possible to engage your students more deeply in the examination of controversy. At Purdue University, students have been asked to apply the critical process and to show how decisions are reached by public officials and others who must choose among imperfect alternatives. The mode for this process is a decision matrix.

The decision matrix developed at Purdue University can be used as an exercise for issues that may not be of primary significance in a particular course, or it can be employed as a way for students to apply the skills that they have developed. This method calls on students to offer possible resolutions to a complex issue. They are asked to speculate on the best possible results and the worst possible results that might follow from adopting either position in the debate. They should state these possible outcomes in a sentence or two at most.

One easily workable form of a *Decision Matrix* is presented as a student handout on page 28. It was created by Brent Slife and Joseph Rubinstein, who were coeditors of *Taking Sides: Psychological Issues* for over 16 years. The matrix has two major positive features. It is easy for the students to demonstrate that they have recognized the major components of the issue, and it is relatively easy to grade. This method also moves the students more clearly into the area of subjective values and can be used to lead into another major use of Taking Sides—highlighting controversy.

Discussing Controversies with Your Students

In addition to drawing upon content-oriented material, critical thinking skills, and subjective values, instructors can use Taking Sides in more formal ways to explore the controversy over critical issues in our society today. It is often not recognized by students that some questions have no "right" or "wrong" answers, merely more or less "considered" opinions. Those people whom we accept as "experts" might merely be giving their opinion on a certain issue, as might those of us with less background in a particular area. This makes the development of critical thinking skills even more important and increases the value of a well-articulated point of view. Students should now be ready for discussion, questioning, and informed debate on important and enduring issues.

Several major systems for discussion and formal debate have been devised for use with Taking Sides. The information that follows is based on long-term experience at Purdue University and Salisbury State College. (Some of the material has been distilled from a detailed manual created for instructors using the Taking Sides volume on psychology.) Many years of refinement in the introductory program at Purdue have produced the system that is presented here. This system is intended for use in discussion groups led by teaching assistants. With modifications, it can be adapted to any classroom setting.

Discussion Modes

These discussion modes are intended as an aid for instructors using *Taking Sides: Psychological Issues* for class discussion; however, the principles contained here are applicable to any of the disciplines covered by Taking Sides volumes. A recommended format for a course that meets three times weekly is to have two formal lectures followed by one discussion session. Here we assume that the discussion sessions supplement the lectures. Included are methods of stimulating and structuring discussions and ways of grading classroom discussions (see **Chapter 3 Evaluation and Grading**).

It should be noted that a number of instructional aids are already provided in the Taking Sides book itself. The introduction to each issue is designed to help students become interested and find relevance in the different issues. The introductions generally are written to provide the necessary background information and to reduce the amount of time that must be devoted to laying the basis for each issue in lectures. In some instances, historical or scientific terms are defined so that they will be easily understood in the context of the selections themselves. Summary postscripts or challenge questions are provided for each issue as well as suggestions for further reading on that particular subject. This may prompt students to do further research and often can add an additional dimension to the debate.

Objectives of Discussion Methods. Although the use of opposing positions for discussion is as old as Socrates, the technique has not been a typical educational strategy in psychology. Usually, students have pens poised ready to collect psychological "facts" rather than to learn of differing points of view. Consequently, you may wish to make a special effort to make clear to the students the function and objectives of the readings. In fact, an explanation of these objectives can itself be a worthwhile discussion of the role of facts, research, values, and conceptual approaches in psychology. The introductions to the Taking Sides volumes, such as "Ways of Looking at Psychological Issues," can be particularly helpful in this regard.

The function of the articles will depend upon you. Course objectives will also vary somewhat with the method or structure of discussion and the grading use. The following *general objectives* for students based on *Taking Sides: Psychological Issues* can thus be modified at your discretion:

1. See the relationship between psychological concepts and controversial issues.
2. Develop sensitivity to the psychological issues that are relevant to the way you structure your life and the decisions you make.
3. Use evidence to work toward a personal resolution of the issues.
4. Clarify your own values.
5. Learn about and from your fellow students.

Preparation for Discussion. Students typically receive little experience in intellectual discussion, especially in leading discussions as some of the methods suggested here demand. There are a number of general steps you can take to facilitate discussion and optimize the benefits received from the dialogue. Providing well-conceived objectives and grading criteria is an important start.

Perhaps as significant, however, is student preparation *before* the discussion. Such preparation consists of many steps. As mentioned earlier, quizzing students on the introduction to Taking Sides or having them identify the "conceptual framework" or "type of information" being used in the articles at hand is excellent preparation for enlightened discussion. Frequent reference to the issues in your lectures can also be very helpful. This permits students to see ties between the text and the upcoming discussion of the issues, and it promotes their application of the text information in the discussion. If discussions are to be student-led or student-structured, a prediscussion meeting between you and the particular student participants can be of enormous benefit. The students' fears and anxieties can be allayed and you can determine what the participants' needs are (references, organization, etc.).

It should be emphasized that some formal structure is usually necessary for productive discussion. Freewheeling dialogue can open the instructor to charges that "we don't need a teacher or a class for that" or "this discussion has nothing to do with the text." A prediscussion meeting gives you, as the instructor, the opportunity to make a strong impact on the process and content while still allowing the class discussion to be student-owned.

Time Management. Another important aspect of structured discussion for the instructor is time management. You need to formulate beforehand and keep strictly to a timetable for the class period to be used effectively.

Time should be allotted in all discussion formats at the beginning and end of the class hour for the instructor. A five-minute lecture at the beginning of the hour can set the stage for discussion by establishing relationships between the text and the readings. Information important to the understanding of the issues may also be dispensed. For instance, in introducing the intelligence issue, you may wish to refresh students' memories on the concepts of reliability and validity.

Five minutes reserved at the end of the discussion will give you an opportunity to provide feedback and closure to the discussion. You may begin by summarizing the main points of the discussion, again emphasizing their relevance to the students and the text. Because the discussion is often ended abruptly due to time constraints, this type of summarization lends some closure to the discussion. You may also wish to comment on the process of the dialogue. Positive aspects of the discussion can be singled out as exemplary. For example, "I thought team 'X' clarified the points of agreement very well." Such feedback is not only valuable to the discussion participants, but it also has the benefit of shaping future discussions.

Panel Discussions

A panel discussion is a very flexible method of involving students in the Taking Sides issues. It can be used as a general didactic strategy for numerous discussions throughout the semester or as a one-shot implementation for a particular issue. It can involve as few as two and as many as ten students directly, and the entire class indirectly. Its use as a general style for conducting dialogues on several issues throughout the semester will be discussed here, as a one-shot implementation will then be self-evident. The following example describes a method that has worked well in introductory psychology classes at Purdue.

Assigning Issues. After discussing the function and objectives of *Taking Sides: Psychological Issues,* ask your students to read the introductory sections of all the issues in the book (or the issues you have preselected) and to make three ordered choices as to which they would prefer to discuss. You might even describe them briefly to stimulate interest. At the next class meeting, try to assign the students to one of their choices as you assign the issues. Remember that as few as two and as many as ten students can handle a single issue. Class size and simple arithmetic should tell you how many would be ideal per issue. If no students are interested in a particular issue you can: a) drop the issue; b) "talk up" the issue and again ask for volunteers; or c) assign people arbitrarily.

In making the assignments, it is important to note which issues will be discussed first. Since these discussions will likely be held very soon, the students should know they will have to prepare quickly. Most students will not have participated in this type of discussion previously and will want to avoid being the first to do so. To encourage participation in the initial discussions, remind the students that doing them early means getting them out of the way. Explain to them that you will give special aid to the first participants, and perhaps even tell them that you will grade these participants less stringently.

With everyone assigned, the next step is to describe the panel discussion structure. The students assigned to each issue are split into two groups, those answering "yes" to the issue and those answering "no." Each group is to begin preparing *now* for a discussion on this issue sometime during the semester (or as indicated on your syllabus). They should not be told whether their position is "yes" or "no" until a week before their discussions are scheduled. However, they should have no difficulty studying until then because they will need to know the opposition's view as well as their own. Anyone not wishing to participate in this format, once it has been described, may do a paper on the issue as described earlier in this manual.

Class Session Structure. The panel discussion consists of four phases: position presentation, position clarification, free-form discussion, and audience response. The process of all of the phases is conducted by you, the moderator.

In the *first phase,* all participants make a short presentation of one aspect of their team position. The purpose of the first phase is twofold: to provide the audience (the rest of the class) with an introduction to the topic and a short statement of the issues involved, and to state positions for the benefit of either team so that the points at issue are clear. The length of each presentation will depend on the number of students on the panel and the time available (approximately a third of the class session for all of the presentations). The teams of panelists outline beforehand the main assertions they wish to make and split them among the team members for presentation. Participants from each team alternate presentations, the first presenter having the primary responsibility of introducing the issue in general. Team members should work together to coordinate their separate presentations.

Each presentation is prepared beforehand, though presenters should be encouraged to make references to previous (and future) presentations for continuity. The individual presentations should begin with a concise statement of the main points the presenter is attempting to assert. This should be followed by a brief summary of the evidence supporting the points, whether logical, empirical, experiential, or expert. One should not dwell, for instance, on the methods used to obtain empirical findings. Only the research conclusions are necessary at this point; the methods may be challenged later. The presentation should then end with a restatement of the primary assertions to again make clear the points being made.

The *second phase* of the panel discussion consists of a question and answer session between the teams. The purpose of this phase is to allow each side to clarify the other team's presentation (or position). Panelists should be instructed that only questions of clarification are appropriate at this juncture: rebuttal and discussion are not permitted. However, this phase does allow each team to begin pinning down the other team as to the specifics of their position. This phase is usually quite short, perhaps five minutes.

The *third phase* is a free-form discussion among panel participants. The first two phases will have warmed up the participants for this phase. Points, counterpoints, rebuttal, and general discussion are all appropriate at this juncture, but panelists should be instructed to deal with the *main issues* as they perceive them. In other words, students should begin the free-form phase with the primary points of disagreement. If argument of trivial points continues for an extended period, the moderator (instructor) simply asks that the participants proceed to another point (e.g., "I think we've exhausted this issue, let's go on to another"). Team members should probably have the main points (and their supporting evidence) they wish to discuss in the free-form phase prepared beforehand. They should also be taking notes during the presentations of the opposition's counterpoints. All team members should be both considerate and willing to dialogue, Any member not actively engaged in discussion can expect a reduced grade, though the quality of what is said, not the quantity, is most important. Approximately half of the total class period is used for this phase.

In the *fourth phase,* the audience simply puts questions and comments to the participants for response. It is important that questions be addressed to specific individuals. First names may be written above the panelists (on the chalkboard) for this purpose. Questions put to the entire group are usually handled by the most vocal member rather than by the member who made the pertinent comment. Some free-form dialogue should be permitted between the audience and panelists, but as many different comments and questions as possible should be encouraged.

Discussion Facilitation. You, as the moderator, should keep a somewhat low profile during this four-phase session. Sitting with the class usually works well. Avoid having the dialogue when participants direct their remarks to you. Statements should be addressed either to fellow participants or to the audience. If, after this instruction, participants continue speaking to you, avoid eye contact with them by looking down. They will gradually direct their eyes elsewhere.

Take extensive notes of the session. (This will be perceived by many students as a rather striking reversal of roles.) Notes should be kept on each individual participant and on the general discussion, both for the purpose of grading and for general feedback.

Following the final phase of the session, provide feedback to the panelists. Most of this feedback should be positive and specific, in order to shape future discussions. Negative comments should be avoided but can be given as general criticism (if not aimed at an individual and preferably only after positive comments). Positive aspects of the discussion can always be found. The feedback period is also an appropriate time to correct any misinformation presented by the panelists. If the students prepare adequately, misinformation will be rare. However, it does happen on occasion and should be corrected immediately in a matter-of-fact manner.

It is very beneficial to meet with both teams just prior to the dialogue. Such a meeting can be very helpful in defining team positions, answering questions, and suggesting references. It is also quite important to review the process (the four phases) as well as the grading criteria. Avoid outlining each team's position if possible; otherwise the students will discuss what they feel you think is important rather than focus on their own thinking. Ask them questions on their own position instead. You might even steer them to think in a "panel discussion" manner. ("If they say _____, what would you say?... But then you [the other team] could say _____," for example.) These preparatory sessions aid the students immensely and usually take no more of your time than typical lecture preparation.

Role-Playing

Students may be asked to play roles in which they simulate the positions of other people, or of themselves, in situations they may have encountered in the past or are likely to encounter in the future. Although it requires some skill on the part of the instructor, this mode has the greatest potential for demonstrating the relevance of textbook information to real-life experiences. It also provides practice in making important decisions and in developing action-oriented human relations skills.

Making Decisions. We recommend that role-playing be used to simulate the forced decisions that characterize life. For example, a student might play the role of a physician or parent required to make important life decisions on the basis of the kind of information available in their text or in *Taking Sides:*

> "Should my patient (or loved one) undergo electroconvulsive therapy to attempt a cure for depression?"

> "As a working parent, should I place my child in day care?"

It has been said that the field of medicine is the art of making decisions on the basis of insufficient evidence. Role-playing can rapidly make it apparent to participants that this art is not unique to medicine.

The role-playing situation has the potential to help each student experience the distinction between possessing absolute truth and using available knowledge to make life decisions. In a well-played role there are no right or wrong answers, but rather the satisfaction of having made a personal decision and the development of confidence that an education can help personal growth.

Varieties of Role-Play Situations. Role-playing can be used in the classroom with any of a number of students, as the following discussion illustrates.

• *SMALL GROUPS.* Some situations lend themselves best to five or six actively involved participants. For example, a family group may be called upon to make a decision about another family member who has severe depression:

> "Should Aunt Jenny undergo the electro-convulsive therapy recommended by her psychiatrist? Should she be placed on a drug treatment program instead, as recommended by a consultant? Should she do neither and continue a program of psychotherapy?"

It is useful with the small group to specify in advance a specific role to be played by each participant. For example: the psychiatrist; the consultant; Aunt Jenny's brother, Mike, who wants to follow the psychiatrist's advice; Mike's wife, who wants to follow the consultant's advice; Aunt Jenny; and other members of the family with advice of their own.

With this procedure, most of the class will act as observers. The participation may come after the role-players have made a decision, if time is set aside for analytic comments and discussion.

Small groups have the advantage of increasing the likelihood that the assigned participants will have prepared well. Often, nonparticipating students who might have found it difficult to role-play for the rest of the class to observe are eager to comment on decisions made by others. For them, this procedure provides good modeling for future role-playing.

• *LARGE GROUPS.* In order to engage all class members as participants, you can simulate a general meeting of activists, such as a PTA meeting, town meeting, or political convention. As instructor, you can then take an active leadership role, such as chairman of the board of education, school principal, PTA president, mayor, chairman of the council, political candidate, or party chair.

As in any large class procedure, it is tempting for many students to remain anonymous. Here are some methods you may use as leader of the meeting to elicit greater participation:

1. Be as mobile within the meeting room as possible. Mentally mark off the room into four quarters. After each contribution, turn to a different quarter of the room expectantly. Be prepared for an occasional silence. Let it develop, unless there is need to clarify the last remark.

2. Be as sensitive as possible to the need for an occasional question or statement from you to calm mounting anxieties or to explain or intensify someone's comment. Playing devil's advocate is often very productive, if done gracefully.

3. Limit your own contribution to that of management. Give participants no hint of what you think concerning proper values or correct decisions. Students should always be convinced that the decisions are theirs to make.

• *BUZZ GROUPS.* Instead of having some students serve as role-players in small groups while others observe, you can break up a large class into a number of small groups operating independently. This procedure has the advantage of keeping everyone actively involved, but it requires some safeguards to prevent confusion and individuals lapsing into silence:

1. Utilize room space optimally. Each group must be tightly confined and as far as possible from other groups. Participants must speak quietly in order to avoid noise interference with other groups.

2. Circulate quietly among the groups. Join in as consultant, when helpful, as long as it does not interfere with the role-playing. For example, you could play the consulting physician for the family deciding what to do for Aunt Jenny.

3. Allow enough time toward the end of the class session for a preassigned spokesperson for each group to give a very brief report.

Time Management. Advance preparation will go a long way toward making each role-play session exciting and productive. Assuming that your class sessions are only 50 minutes long, allowing enough time for an end-of-session conclusion is likely to be your most serious problem.

Your students should be convinced in advance that role-playing is no joke, that there will always be a specific agenda, and that you will serve as timekeeper. Assure them in advance that once the role-playing session begins, *there will be no breaking of roles.* You, of course, must also resist the temptation. In general, breaking out of role wastes time. Assure students that you will be happy to answer any questions about the next role-playing session outside of class, but not during the actual session.

There should be no ambiguity about the decision to be made. The nature of the decision should cue students about the information they should gather and comprehend in advance. They should consider what alternative decisions can be made, discuss the alternatives in terms of information and personal values, and then *decide.* A reasonable agenda for each role-playing session might be as follows:

1. (5 minutes) A quiz or mini-lecture concerning terms or concepts relating text materials to the current issue.
2. (20 to 30 minutes) The actual role-played event.
3. (10 minutes) For small groups: observer analysis and comment. For buzz groups: individual group reports.
4. (5 minutes) Instructor summary and feedback. Some suggested comments:

"In preparation for this class you had decided to focus on..."
"Today you first considered the following information..." "Then you proceeded to..."
"Some of you decided to..."
"While others among you..."
"The final consensus was to. . ."
"In general, I felt that you did an excellent job of taking all the variables we are familiar with into consideration and coming to grips with the decision."
"I felt that you faltered somewhat in considering some variables."

5. Depending on your total course setup, you might need to allow some time to prepare for the next issue.

More on Buzz Groups

The buzz-group method has the primary advantage of requiring very little formal preparation on the part of the students. It is important that students read the articles in *Taking Sides* as well as any pertinent text materials, but no presentations or positions need be formulated beforehand. Most of the preparation, in fact, belongs to the instructor. Have the students bring all text and *Taking Sides* material to class with them.

The typical buzz-group technique is to split the class arbitrarily into small groups and assign each group an objective. This technique can be adapted to *Taking Sides:*

Psychological Issues by assigning the point-counterpoints from the issue introductions as objectives, the number of such point-counterpoints to dictate the number and size of the groups. Usually a total of six or eight students in a group is optimal. You may wish to add to or omit from the point-counterpoints listed in the issue introductions in *Taking Sides: Psychological Issues.* (Note: Only Taking Sides: Psychology Titles have point-counterpoints.)

The general goal of all groups is to explain, support, and illustrate one or more point-counterpoints involved in the issue at hand. Each member of the group will have particular responsibilities toward this end. One way to distribute group responsibilities is as follows: One person is the introducer of the point-counterpoint; two people are the summarizers of each side of the point-counterpoint; two more people cite the support evidence for each side of the point-counterpoint; one other person illustrates the point-counterpoint; and two more people perform the function of fielding any questions pertinent to the point-counterpoint or presentations by the other group members. We suggest that each of the roles be more fully described in a handout for the students to read. Professor Brent Slife and Professor Joseph Rubinstein created the *Role Description for Informal Debates* (p. 29) for their students at Purdue University. Please note that although it refers to point-counterpoints, a unique feature to Taking Sides: Psychology Titles, it can easily be adapted to any Taking Sides volume. (You may want to omit certain roles or combine them, depending on the group size. You may also wish to prepare an additional handout that helps each group member fulfill his or her role in relation to the specific objective.)

You may either give the groups a short period of time to decide who assumes each role or use a "count off" to arbitrarily distribute the roles—ones are introducers, twos are summarizers for the "yes," threes are summarizers for the "no," and so on. When the assignments are made and the role-description handouts are distributed, it would be helpful to describe the roles in more detail. Once you think students understand their responsibilities, assign a point-counterpoint (or set of point-counterpoints) and have them begin work on it. Ten minutes is usually all that is required for this type of buzz session. Your role at this time is to move from group to group to observe and assist where needed.

When all groups are ready, each member makes a very short presentation (perhaps 30 seconds, depending on the time available) with the exception of the fielders, who "field" one or two quick questions. You may wish to give some feedback to each group as they finish in order to shape future presentations and correct any misinformation. Students in the other groups should be encouraged to be attentive and ask questions. A pop quiz from your notes on the presentations usually ensures attention and participation.

Teaching Through Formal Debate

Structured discussion in class can naturally lead to the most formal method for using Taking Sides: the formal debate. This method requires students to synthesize everything they have learned to this point and to present a coherent, well-researched, well-supported position before classmates and instructor. The articles themselves have been selected to provide as much material as possible for debate, both in terms of content and forcefulness of presentation. Debates may well expose differences and similarities in the arguments more clearly than written assignments can.

Although formal methods are presented here, debates can also be more informal, if appropriate for a particular issue. An expository debate can be created simply by asking two students to come to class prepared to discuss the issue at the next meeting. This form of debate may take no more than a few minutes and will leave you free to amplify or detract from either argument. Whether formal or informal, debates have many advantages:

- They force students to speak in front of their peers (a beneficial college experience).
- They force students to adopt a point of view and defend their position—as they may well have to do in the real world.
- Debates, with the provided text materials, are fairly well outlined and may require a minimum of student
- research in order to successfully defend a position.
- Debates relieve you of extensive lecture preparation and give students responsibility for generating their own learning experience.
- Debates allow issues to move freely into areas not necessarily covered by the text materials.
- Debates are excellent formats for group discussion and are easily adapted to situations where teaching assistants are responsible for discussion groups outside of the standard classroom lecture.
- Debates give students a role and structure in which to express opinions that may differ from the instructor's.

Two methods for formal debates are presented here. The first was designed as an additional mode by psychology professors Joseph Rubinstein and Brent Slife for Purdue University. This is an extension of their discussion modes, which were presented in detail in the discussion section. For further reference on formal debates, see Robert C. Dick, *Argumentation and Rational Debating* (William C. Brown, 1972).

Formal Debate

Debate involves having specified class members form teams to test competitively two sides of an issue. The remainder of the class can then vote for the most convincing team. The assignment and organization of students into debate teams can be similar to that of the panel discussion.

The procedure in debate begins with a proposed solution to a problem. A series of carefully timed, formal, spoken arguments are then alternated between an affirmative speaker and a negative speaker. If some members of the class have had experience with formal debating, you might do well to have them assume some responsibility for procedural management and timing.

Propositions. The *proposition* is the statement being debated. It is stated affirmatively and conclusively, much in the manner of a scientific hypothesis. A debatable proposition is considered to be one of three types: fact, value, or policy. An effective debater can spot the type of proposition he or she must work with and determine what its specific demands are.

• *FACT.* Propositions of fact state that a phenomenon is true or false—for example, "Several modern religious cults use brainwashing techniques to convert young people." (In this case, it might be useful to delimit the proposition by naming a specific religious group.)

Fact propositions demand that the proponent:

1. Assert some externally established criteria of definition, rule, or law generally agreed upon as the basis of fact—"The techniques of brainwashing consist of. . . ."

2. Demonstrate that the phenomenon in question is consistent with the criteria—"X and Y religious groups use the following brainwashing techniques to convert young people."

• *VALUE.* Propositions of value state that a phenomenon is consistent with criteria for evaluating its acceptability—for example, "Psychology can best improve the human condition by directing its efforts toward controlling human behavior."

Value propositions demand that the proponent:

1. Convince the audience that the proponent's own criteria of personal values are acceptable—"The human condition will be improved when everyone is happy and productive."

2. Convince the audience that acceptable criteria of value are fulfilled by the phenomenon in question—"Psychology now has within its grasp the means to make everyone happy and productive."

• *POLICY.* Propositions of policy call for some form of action. In general, they may contain some elements of both fact and value. They are often recognizable by use of the word *should* and must speculate about the consequences of the action—for example, "As a national policy we should eliminate all forms of violence from television programming."

Policy propositions demand that the proponent convince the audience that the opposed action will be beneficial "When violence on TV is eliminated, violence in our streets will diminish."

Note that although most of the issues contained in *Taking Sides: Psychological Issues* lend themselves to one or another type of proposition, some may be treated as

you choose. One issue may ask, for example, "Should Animals Be Used in Psychological Research?" Possible propositions may be as follows:

Fact: "Experiments using animals are essential to the development of many life-saving medical procedures."

Value: "Animal experimentation benefits both humans and animals."

Policy: "Experimental treatments should always be tested on animals before they are tested on humans."

Argument. The *argument* consists of using both facts and opinions as evidence in the logical analysis of a proposition to enable judges to arrive at a decision. It is essential that all team members be thoroughly familiar with the opposing side's argument. They must be able to select those arguments that are pertinent to the proposition and reject those that are irrelevant in providing rebuttal to the opposing team's evidence.

An excellent preparation would be for students to make a list of points of agreement and disagreement for the two teams. *(Note that a large number of the multiple-choice questions in the individual instructor's manuals are specifically oriented toward points of agreement and disagreement.)* Points of disagreement should be stated so that the affirmative side can unambiguously say "yes" to it and the negative side can clearly say "no."

Debate Format. There are generally two types of format: the traditional and the cross-examination. Each format may have two or three members for each side. At the introductory level, we recommend that you stay with the traditional format, since the cross-examination format requires more debating skill, is more complicated, and takes longer.

In the traditional format, each constructive speech is usually given eight minutes and each rebuttal speech is usually given four minutes. However, you will need buffer time for the class to vote and for you to add a few words of your own at the close of the class session. Be sure to work out your timing in advance and stick to your schedule.

Traditional Format

Constructive speeches:
1. First affirmative
2. First negative
3. Second affirmative
4. Second negative

Rebuttal speeches:
1. First negative
2. First affirmative
3. Second negative
4. Second affirmative

The vote

More on the Debate Format

The following formal debate plan has been used in many advanced courses that follow the introductory psychology course but can easily be integrated into a first course especially if it is the type of class that utilizes discussion sessions as well as formal lectures.

First, be advised that students are wary of this form of education, and they will have to know what you expect of them. In order to convey this, you may wish to create a handout similar to *Preparing for a Formal Debate* on page 30, created by Professor Dan Gallagher, Salisbury State University, which describes roles and rules for debates. The major roles that seem sufficient are those of *stater, prover,* and *attacker.* A given debate will thus involve six students: a stater, a prover, and an attacker on each side of the Taking Sides issue.

Stater. The stater for any given issue will start the discussion, stating how the "yes" or "no" side views the issue. This introduction is generally brief, possibly only going as far as presenting and explaining the introductory material given in the issue introductions and postscripts. The stater may have prepared notes but should be advised that this is a conversation, not a reading experience. This role generally takes from two to five minutes, depending on the student and the complexity of the point of view.

Prover. The prover is possibly the most difficult role. This student must bring up relevant research to back up the statements made by the stater. He or she must have good knowledge of the position and must understand the assigned article—facts, opinions, and other elements—in order to do well. This may take from five to 15 minutes, depending on the depth of proof. The prover may also be encouraged to use outside sources to strengthen the arguments. An opinion survey may be in order. The prover should be aware that his or her facts and data may be disputed later and should be prepared to defend his or her empirical sources when the attacker speaks.

Attacker. The attacker is responsible for leading the arguments against the other team. His or her research may be minimal, but he or she will be required to listen well, think quickly, ferret out logical flaws and opinions that are disguised as facts, and question the empiricism of quoted materials. The attacker should be well prepared and have read the opposite side of the issue.

The students should think of these as roles. Attacks should not be made on personal attributes of the participants but on the merits of the prepared presentations and the ideas put forth in the issues.

A given debate thus might consist of the following exchanges between pro and con teams:

"Yes" team—The stater brings forth the propositions of the "yes" side of the issue.

"Yes" team—The prover from the "yes" side backs up the stater.

"No" team—The stater from the "no" side puts forth the team's perception of the issue.

"No" team—The prover from the "no" side shows why the stater holds this position with facts and data.

"Yes" team—The attacker from the "yes" side may direct several questions to the other side or point out errors noted in the issue as presented.

"No" team—The attacker from the "no" team gets a chance to do the same.

Other formats are possible. For example, the "yes" stater may be immediately followed by the "no" stater. Then the two provers can take their turns. Either side may go first; this can be determined by a coin toss or by your decision as to which side should logically initiate the debate.

Audience. The students in the class not directly participating in the debate have two roles. They may serve as further attackers, after the team attackers have finished, and they may serve as part of the grading and evaluation process (**see Chapter 3 Evaluation and Grading**).

Instructor. You will do well to stay out of the debates. Once the debate has begun, no further interference is necessary. Often the students will have prepared trains of thought, and interruptions may spoil the points that they are developing. After the attackers have finished, you may wish to pursue Issues.

It is strongly suggested that you not reveal any biases on either side of these issues. Your biases would inhibit students who think they are defending a position that you do not support. After the debate is over, you may wish to influence the class conclusion, but this should be reserved until the end.

Two forms of "interruption" are acceptable and often necessary during debates. These may be used by debaters on the other team, by the members of the debate audience, or by the instructor.

• Clarification. This may be requested by anyone who is not certain of what a presenter has said. It may be asked for if a student is uncertain how a research study supported the issue or how a study was done, or questions may be raised in relation to any other point of misunderstanding. Clarifications should not be used as an attack device, however.

• Question. This may be employed by any nondebater at any time after the major arguments have been made. Theoretically, the attacker on the opposite panel should be asking the questions, but the audience also has this right (after, of course, allowing the attacker enough time to develop his or her line of interrogation).

Again, these roles are clearly defined in the student handout *Preparing for a Formal Debate*; it is suggested that the handout be duplicated and made available to the students long before any debate.

Assigning Debates. Students generally have formed opinions concerning these important issues before formal study takes place. They bring these opinions with them from their previous schooling or experiences in the world. These opinions are often useful to you, and you may assign students to a debate team based on what they already feel is the "right" answer on a particular issue.

Students may also have a preference based on their interest in a particular topic from the text. Within reason, it is a good idea to take advantage of students' interests. Their efforts will generally be greater if they are doing something that is important to them. You may find it beneficial to let students select both the topic they wish to debate and the position they wish to defend. Professor Kurt Finsterbusch, Department of Sociology, University of Maryland, surveys his students this way early in the semester. We have his *Debate Preference Survey* on page 31 of the student handouts section. All students are required to read the introductions to all the issues and indicate their preferences on the survey. After the survey forms are collected, it is a fairly simple matter to collate the requests. Most students' preferences can be accommodated. You may find that some issues elicit no interest for a given class. In this case, you may elect to skip that issue or use one of the other methods for issue analysis.

An alternative plan for assigning debates is to simply have students sign up for a particular debate regardless of their reasons for preferring one topic over another. Before submitting the sign-up sheet to students, the instructor might want to add dates to the debates, since that may often be a factor in favoring one topic over another.

Simple Debate Format. For those instructors who are convinced of the value of debate but are limited in terms of time or other resources, a simple debate format has been developed at Howard Community College. This method uses a variation of the traditional debate. This variation has some distinct advantages over the total involvement of the formal methods. The simple debate does not necessarily require the entire class period and can allow for the coverage of other material or emphasis on a particular aspect of the discussion. The simple debate requires less preparation time on the part of the

instructor and can be less intimidating for the students. A simple debate system can be created using the student handout *Guidelines and Format for the Simple Debate* on page 32, which was developed by Professor Larry Madaras, Department of History, Howard Community College, and designed to be handed out to students early in the course.

Summary of Major Steps Involved in a Complete Formal Debate Method

The flowchart in Appendix 4 shows a summary of the steps necessary for the formal debates using the class surveys to assess student topic preferences. Topics are then assigned. All students are required to read the opposing issues before the debate date (less formal methods may be applied at this stage). A quiz or lecture might be given prior to a debate on the assigned day. After the debate, the class surveys may be collected, students' grades may be determined, and the data may be collated by any computational method chosen. Feedback in the form of grades and comments may then be given at the next class. Final grades may be determined by averaging grades earned in each debate.

This system may seem at first glance to entail a lot of effort, and it *does* require advance planning. However, once the ground rules have been explained to the students, they generally perform pretty well. You might be wise to select several of the better students in a class for the first debate so that a "good" example may be set. Give appropriate feedback—let students know what they did well and, in a graceful fashion, what they did poorly. After two or three debates, the method falls into a rhythm, and they are easily run.

A Final Note

Debates and other methods are not mutually exclusive. One topic may be best handled by less formal methods, others by debates; or students not debating may be required to report on an issue via issue reports or analysis reports (provided as Student Handouts). Let the importance of an issue, your student population, and your goals as a teacher guide you as you select methods. Any of them are valuable as you help students arrive at personal conclusions.

CHAPTER 3

EVALUATION AND GRADING

No matter which of the techniques outlined in **Part 1 Background and Basics** seem most appropriate for your needs, an important issue for any teaching strategy is evaluation. The instructor's manual provided with each individual Taking Sides volume will be of help to you in choosing testing and evaluation techniques, as will the following evaluative systems. These systems can simplify the evaluation process and protect both you and your students against involuntary bias in dealing with some very subjective areas. The first method is derived from material created at Purdue University for use with discussion modes and debates. The second is a more elaborate system, in use at Salisbury State College.

Emphasize Process Over Content

Performance appraisal of debates and discussions can be done subjectively or objectively, with large or small classes, much as with other teaching approaches. Subjective assessment need not be very dissimilar from term paper or essay grading, while objective evaluation may be conducted by the usual means, such as multiple-choice, true/false, and short answer questions.

In order to promote constructive student dialogue, do not emphasize assessing the amount of the course materials retained by each student, but rather how the student uses the course materials. Thus, your interest will be not so much the factual content of the discussion or debate, but the process of the discussion and students' thinking. The students, too, will be encouraged by the challenge of emphasizing process over content.

In a panel discussion, for example, upgrade students who provide empirical evidence for their arguments, anticipate the opposition's points and are ready with counterpoints, evaluate the reasoning and support of the opposition, and the like. Upgrading is merited because the content of the arguments or points are the students', not necessarily the text's, the article's, or the instructor's, although all of these sources provide necessary guidance.

In this case, since the students are relatively free of content evaluation (in favor of process—that is, the "how" rather than the "what"), they will be more willing to focus and apply their own thinking, relate the issues to their own lives, and question the supposed facts more openly.

Grading for all projects and activities may be based on the following possible evaluation criteria:

- Use of supporting materials outside of the Taking Sides readings
- Grasp of the issue and important related points
- Proper use of supporting empirical evidence
- Realization of points of agreement and points of disagreement
- The ability to anticipate and counter opposing viewpoints
- Use of supporting points not suggested by Taking Sides introductions
- The ability to see and challenge flaws in the opposition's arguments and research as well as one's own flaws
- Use of constructive criticism and rationales
- The ability to make the topic relevant to the audience and/or opposition (if there is one)
- The ability to anticipate questions
- The ability to ask appropriate questions

Grading

One method of grading is to quantify the components of a good debate with some rating scale in order to confer a composite grade. Professor Neil Sapper, Department of Social Sciences, Amarillo College, uses a *Debate Evaluation Form* (p. 33) to grade his students' debates. Components may be dropped or added to suit the instructor's debate format and requirements. For example, Professor Sapper adds an "annotation" line under the written components, which refers to his requirement that each student provide an annotated photocopy of one page from each outside source that is utilized in preparation for debate. This form is also universal to all Taking Sides volumes.

You can apply your rating scale to a group team (and thus assign all members of the group the same grade) or apply the criteria to individual participants. Your choice may be governed by the format of the particular activity or discussion. Things you might be looking for in each item in your rating scale include the following:

- Did the group or student prepare well, recognizing the primary issues and gathering and assessing the appropriate supporting materials?
- Was the team presentation well organized and effective?
- How interesting was the project, discussion, debate, or presentation? A lackluster job may indicate a poor understanding of the issue or little preparation and effort.

- Was the issue presented and defended empirically?
- Did the student or group of students go beyond the issue as presented in the Taking Sides volume? Students who can relate their topic to the bigger issue should get credit for their vision.
- Was the group or student perceptive to the weak points on the opposite side?
- How well did the students work together to achieve the goals of the activity?

Another option, which allows the instructor to evaluate the students who are not debating and to make use of students' responses to the debaters, was developed by Professor James M. Kilbride, Department of Psychology, Miami-Dade Community College South. His *Issue Evaluation Form* handout is presented on page 36 and may be used in conjunction with any of the previously described Taking Sides discussion/debate techniques that involve student presentations. This handout should be distributed to nondebating students at the time the issue is assigned. The students may then fill in the appropriate information at the appropriate times. Hence, line 1 would be filled in before the selections are read, lines 2 and 3.a and 3.b after both readings have been completed, questions for presenters during the debate, and the conclusion and evaluation lines directly after the debate or presentation. The instructor may then collect the completed forms and determine how well the student internalized the readings and how much attention the student accorded the debate. Then the instructor may apply the student evaluations toward the debaters' scores.

Most students recognize the purpose of peer grading of group activities. It forces students to work together in groups and to prepare outside of class. Partial responsibility for the grades of others also motivates students to perform well.

PART 2

Student Handouts

QUESTIONS TO ASK WHEN EXAMINING A POSITION

It is vital to learn how to evaluate an argument calmly and objectively. Discussing the following questions will help. These questions will enable you to break down an argument into its component parts, thereby avoiding the common tendency to be swayed by a presenter's delivery techniques or by one's own set of biases and opinions.

• Question: *How Empirical Is the Presentation?*

The most persuasive argument is the one that supports its thesis by referring to relevant, accurate, and up-to-date data from the best sources possible. One should investigate the credibility of the author, how recent the material is, the type of research (if any) that supports the position outlined, and the degree of documentation behind any argument. Empiricism implies going to the best source for material. This suggests that original research material is preferable to secondary sources, which in turn are preferable to hearsay.

• Question: *What Is Fact? What Is Opinion?*

A *fact* is a statement that can be proven. In contrast, an *opinion* is a statement that expresses how a person feels about an issue or what someone thinks is true. Many authors blend fact and opinion; it is the responsibility of the critical thinker to discriminate successfully between the two.

This process of discrimination often ties in with the concept of empiricism. Facts are generally empirically determined from research. They are documented and can be known or observed by other people. Facts can be verified in other sources or can be replicated by other research. Good facts should be most convincing in any issue.

Opinions should carry less weight in evaluating an argument. While the writer may believe them to be true, opinions are a product of the writer's biases and personal system of beliefs. While many opinions make good sense and may win a reader's approval, they must still be classified as mere opinions if there is no factual evidence supporting them. Opinion may, in fact, be entirely correct, but generally it still should be viewed with less trust than facts.

Some statements contain both fact and opinion. For example, research has demonstrated that animals living in crowded cages show more aggressive behavior than those living in less crowded cages. A statement such as "Overcrowding of people in slum areas will foster

high levels of aggression, rape, and child abuse in the same way that one sees in caged animals" contains elements of both opinion and fact.

• Question: *What Propaganda Is Being Used?*

Propaganda is information presented in order to influence a reader. It is not necessarily "good" or "bad." Many authors consciously use propaganda techniques in order to convince their readers of their special point of view. A close look at the author's background or some of the motivations and editorial policies of the source of the publication may provide clues about what types of propaganda techniques might be used.

• Question: *What Cause/Effect Relationships Are Proposed?*

Much material is written to establish or advance a hypothesis that some circumstances "cause" specific things to happen. Experiments often consist of searching for cause/effect relationships. Scientists seem to be linking more and more observations with their antecedent causes. Students should note when an issue has at its heart a disputed cause/effect relationship; isolating the claim and examining the relationship is the readers' responsibility.

• Question: *Are These Cause/Effect Relationships Merely Correlations?*

Many cause/effect statements are flawed because no appropriate research or evidence has isolated a single cause. There may be other hidden factors underlying the relationship. A good example is this statement: "Birds fly south in winter because it gets cold in northern areas." This statement is plausible, and many readers would accept it because it "makes sense." Data exist to show a relationship between temperature and bird population density: population decreases as temperature decreases. However, no experiment has conclusively established that temperature is a causative factor of bird migration. Alternative hypotheses may very well also explain the behavior. Food supplies may become scarce during low-temperature periods, breeding instincts may precipitate migration, or the birds may simply want a change of scenery! If sufficiently controlled experiments could rule out these alternative hypotheses, the cause/effect statement could be made. As it is, a simple correlation (statement of coincidence) is all that remains: "Birds fly south at the same time that the weather turns cold." It would even be possible (although not very plausible) with the observed data to infer the opposite causation: "It turns cold in the northern latitudes because the body heat from migrating birds is no longer present!"

Students should be made aware that faulty cause/effect statements may be a major source of confusion and misdirection used by authors to defend their points of view. In some cases, the faulty cause/effect proposition is the only rationale used by an author. A good technique for analyzing this sort of error is to have the students try to generate alternative plausible hypotheses for any proposed cause/effect relationship.

• Question: *Is Information Distorted?*

Many authors, in an attempt to produce facts to substantiate their positions, quote statistics and research that support their viewpoints. All of these statements of facts may be biased. "Statistics don't lie—statisticians do" is a truism. Students should always question the bias involved in obtaining and presenting data. If averages are given, ranges and standard deviations should be evaluated critically. One interesting question that can be raised is: What statistics or data are missing? If a simple survey could be done (in lieu of a statement such as "Most Americans believe that . . ."), why was such an easily supportable piece of data not produced?

Students should learn not to be too easily impressed by statistical data. Tabulated numbers or graphs may only reflect opinions.

• Question: *Are Analogies Faulty?*

Many authors make much of analogies as they attempt to prove their theses. An *analogy* is a comparison of a hypothesis (which is unproven) to a known set of causal events. For example, a statement such as "The United States should not be getting involved in Iraq's politics; we will have another fiasco as we did in Vietnam" uses an analogy. However true the second part of the sentence may or may not be, it should not necessarily be accepted as a demonstration of the truth of the first part of the sentence. Analogies usually ignore many differences (in this example, differences in military position, geographic location, political motivation, and other fac-

tors) that make the current situation unsuitable for comparison and render the analogy worthless.

• Question: *Is the Author Oversimplifying the Issue?*

Authors generally try to show their theses in the best possible light and to discredit opposing positions. When authors are so single-minded as to completely ignore opposite positions, they probably are guilty of over-simplification.

It may be argued, for example, that bilingual education has been shown to be beneficial for students. However, if data are presented without a discussion (even a derogatory discussion) of the many social ramifications of bilingual education programs, the argument has not answered all of the important questions.

• Question: *Is the Author Stereotyping?*

This sort of logical flaw is similar to the cause/effect flaw. The authors may have observed some general behavior; they then may attempt to apply this general behavior (which may or may not be true) to a specific individual or situation. For example, if an author asserts that American cars are inferior to foreign cars (which may or may not be true), he or she might not establish that any *particular* American car is truly inferior. Each point should be analyzed as it is empirically observed, not as it is grouped with other observations.

• Question: *Are There Faulty Generalizations?*

In the case of a faulty generalization, a judgment is based on inaccurate or incomplete information. For example: "Ducks and geese migrate south for the winter; therefore, all birds migrate south for the winter."

In presentations, many subtle forms of inappropriate generalizations may occur. The most common form concerns research in one area being applied to other areas (as in faulty analogy). For example: "The brain deals in electric potentials. Computers deal with electric potentials. We can thus say that the brain is a computer."

Another example of a faulty generalization is when an author observes only one event or cites only one case study and infers that this applies to many other phenomena. Sigmund Freud could be considered guilty of this—his theories of behavior are derived from only a few published observations of individual case studies.

PROPAGANDA ALERT

Critical thinking requires you to be actively involved with your reading assignments. The following is a list of some of the more commonly used propaganda techniques, which is derived from *Analyzing Controversy: An Introductory Guide* by Gary K. Clabaugh, La Salle University, and Edward G. Rozycki, Widener University (Contemporary Learning Series, 1997). Be on the alert for those as you read the Taking Sides debates.

Generalization

One kind of generalization that can be hard to identify, interpret, or test is the reification. To reify means to treat a vague general term as if it were a concrete, even living, thing. Reifications tend to obscure important questions about responsibility, cost, and benefit. In addition, they are frequently used to demean or demonize entire groups of people.

We encounter reifications every day. Below are some headlines from a major metropolitan newspaper with possible reifications italicized.

- *Drug Company* Did Not Act on AIDS Virus Warning
- *City* and *Union* Extend Strike Deadline
- *Chinese Police* Detain Wife of Political Prisoner
- Clinton Calls on *UN* to Cut Back on Waste

These are story headlines, and, in most cases, in the body of the story, we learn who in the drug company failed to act, which city and union officials extended the strike deadline, and so forth. Sometimes, however, these vital details never emerge.

Consider a column we found on the commentary page of a local newspaper with the headline: "UN should clean up its act." The columnist charges that"... *the UN's bureaucracy* has long ago forsaken its commitment to Article 100 of the [UN] Charter." (Article 100 forbids UN staffers from seeking or receiving instructions from any government.) He denounces *"UN apparatchiks [who] have tried to cover their trail . . ."* and charges that *"The UN bureaucracy . . .* inhabits a culture of paranoia, fearful always that a powerful member country or a powerful block of countries is looking over their shoulder" [stress added.] There are over 20,000 UN employees working worldwide at many different jobs, but the reader is encouraged to lump them all together as "apparatchiks" (a derisive term for Soviet-era bureaucrats) and "the UN bureaucracy." Some UN employees may well deserve such labels; but most must surely be worthy and do admirable work. Consider, as an example, those who sacri-

ficed their lives attempting to bring food and medicine to besieged Bosnians. Do they deserve such labels?

Name Calling

Many people would not directly insult those who disagree with them. Such people often pride themselves on either their civility or objectivity. Nonetheless, they often subtly insult their opponents not by focusing on the argument but by questioning their opponents' character or motives.

In evaluating competing sides of a controversial issue, look for terms that delegitimate interests (rob them of their legitimacy). Whose interests they invalidate can be quite revealing. For example, in "The Tilt to the News: How American Journalism Has Swerved from the Ideal of Objectivity, "The *World and I* (December 1993), H. Joachim Maitre denounces the alleged liberality of National Public Radio (NPR). He cites as an example NPR's correspondent at the Supreme Court, Nina Totenberg, for her "stubborn effort to prevent Clarence Thomas from being confirmed as a justice of the Court." He might have said "intensive," "tireless," or "persistent" effort. "Stubborn" delegitimates her actions without giving reasons as to why he thinks she was wrong.

Emotions and Persuasion

However irrelevant they might be when it comes to factual claims or the logic of an argument, feelings still play a particularly crucial role in persuasion. In fact, Aristotle classified emotional appeals (pathos) as one of the most effective means of influencing others.

Some appeals to emotion are uncalculated, coming from disputants who are emotionally wrapped up in the issue themselves. But others emanate from practiced publicists or cunning propagandists who play on emotions as skillfully as a virtuoso plays the piano. We should be wary of this. Some classic appeals to emotion that you should watch out for follow.

Appeals to Fear

Fear as a self-protective response is perfectly reasonable. But this same emotion can also cloud judgment. And, as in the case of envy, fear can be played upon.

Some possible indicators that fear is being appealed to are the use the fear (F) terms instead of the more neutral (N) terms in the following pairs: (F) bully (N) assertive; (F) aggressive (N) self-confident; (F) sneaky (N) cautious; (F) underhanded (N) circumspect; (F) furtive (N) discreet; (F) surreptitious (N) watchful; (F) out-of-control (N) spontaneous; (F) impulsive (N) freewheeling; (F) rash (N) instinctive; (F) reckless (N) carefree. The point is that the same essential trait or behavior can be referred to in a way that plays on our feelings, in this case, fear.

Appeals to Hatred

Hatred is strangely seductive, and zealots of every stripe seem to need a devil. Hitler, for instance, demonized the Jews, and it served Stalin's murderous purposes to incite hatred for "wreckers" (of the revolution) and so-called enemies of the people.

Loaded language is particularly effective in triggering hate. For example, there seems to be a nearly endless supply of nasty words that promote and exploit hatred for particular racial, ethnic, or religious groups. These are all too commonly known, so we prefer not to provide any further examples for the sake of good taste. Bear in mind, however, that there are subtler loaded words that also play on hatred. Here are some code words used to trigger revulsion: welfare queen, bleeding heart, fascist, extremist, international banker, one-worlder, tree-hugger, union buster, puritan, bureaucrat, shyster, and draft dodger. Of course, there are many, many more.

Appeals to Pride

Pride is another of the so-called seven deadly sins, the one, we are told, that most surely separates a sinner from the grace of God. Often we can spot appeals to pride by looking for characteristic indicator phrases like the following:

- Any educated (or substitute intelligent, healthy) person knows that . . .
- A person with your good background (breeding) can't help but see that . . .
- You will be proud to know that . . .

An inverse appeal to pride plays on our fear of seeming stupid. Persuasion professionals are well aware of this and cleverly use it to their advantage. To make you feel alone and stupid in your opinions, for instance, they might commission a poll with loaded questions; then release the findings to the press. Essentially they are saying "Look at all the people who agree with us. You must be wrong." Be alert for such maneuvers.

Slogans

Slogans are vague statements that typically are used to express positions or goals. They characteristically conceal potential conflict while promoting broad but only shallow consensus. Because of their vagueness, they are easy to agree with; but we often later find that others interpret them in ways we find objectionable.

Slogans are not so vague as to be meaningless. On the contrary, slogans are powerful persuaders precisely because they do mean something. Crucially, however, what that something is differs dramatically from person to person.

Consider the following:

- Statements difficult to disagree with: "Take a bite out of crime!"; "Support our troops!"; "Preserve the environment!"; "Just say 'No!' to drugs!"
- Key terms with multiple interpretations: "law" in "The law is too soft on criminals" and "peace" in "peacekeeping force" or "peace-loving nations."
- Statements commonly used at political rallies: the "New Deal," "Contract with America," or "with liberty and justice for all."
- Statements used by the media: "The Trial of the Century," "Deficit Reduction," "Liberals," and "Conservatives."

Pseudo Solutions

When a real solution to an urgent problem is not forthcoming, many arguers offer pseudo solutions, vague generalizations that sound convincing and incite people to a cause but say little more than "Let's solve this problem by doing something that will solve this problem." That's pretty safe advice, but with these solutions, arguers are really avoiding the possibility of failure, evading details, and neglecting to talk about who will shoulder the cost. Real solution proposals, on the other hand, require the risk of failure, saying exactly what is to be done, and, often as not, wrestling with issues of cost.

To distinguish pseudo solutions from potentially workable ones, use the "Can it fail?" Rule. This involves asking, Can the solution fail?

1. *No* identifies pseudo solutions.
2. *Yes* identifies real possibilities.

Consider the following problems and paired "solutions." The "a" items are pseudo solutions. The "b" items are real proposals. Can you see why?

1. That party is too noisy.
   a. Quiet it down.
   b. Call the cops.
2. Kids aren't doing homework.
   a. Motivate them.
   b. Assign lunch detentions.
3. Trains are seldom on time.
   a. Improve on-time performance.
   b. Purchase more locomotives.
4. Government is wasting money.
   a. Improve fiscal efficiency.
   b. Decentralize purchasing.
5. Too many children are using illegal drugs.
   a. Teach them to say "No!" to drugs.
   b. Spend 10 percent more on drug education.

Presuppositions

Controversies may rest—not on deliberate misinformation—but on the incorrect assumption that the fundamental sources of knowledge that we depend on are functioning well. It is this presupposition of their trustworthiness that supports our arguments. For instance, consider the following presupposition shared by disputants on either side of the controversy Should Laws Prohibiting Marijuana Use Be Relaxed? from *Taking Sides Drugs and Society,* Seventh edition (Contemporary Learning Series, 2005). Ethan Nadelmann, founder and executive director of the Drug Policy Foundation, argues that law enforcement officials are overzealous in prosecuting individuals for marijuana possession. Eighty-seven per-cent of marijuana arrests are for possession of small amounts of the drug. The Office of National Drug Control Policy (ONDCP) contends that marijuana is not a harmless drug. Besides causing physical problems, marijuana affects academic performance and emotional adjustment. Underlying both of their arguments is the presupposition that adults cannot be permitted to make their own decisions about the use of particular drugs as they choose. A libertarian who worries about governmental restrictions on personal liberty would immediately recognize this deep assumption and challenge it. The point here is that controversies rest on presuppositions that may in themselves be challenged.

TAKING SIDES ISSUE REPORT

Name: _____

Course: _____

State the issue in your own words:

State the pro position:

State the con position:

Indicate three main areas of disagreement:

From library or web research, state two other positions:

State your position; justify:

Indicate where information pertinent to this issue is discussed in the text:

Discuss the issue utilizing critical thinking skills:

List new vocabulary:

TAKING SIDES ANALYSIS REPORT (LONG FORM)

Name: _____

Course: _____

Book: _____

Issue number: _____ Title of issue: _____

1. Author and major thesis of the *Yes* side. _____
_____
_____

2. Author and major thesis of the *No* side. _____
_____
_____

3. What fallacies of question-framing are made by the authors of the text? _____
_____
_____

4. Briefly state in your own words two facts presented by each side. _____
_____
_____
_____
_____
_____

5. Briefly state in your own words two opinions presented by each side. _____
_____
_____
_____
_____
_____

6. Briefly identify as many fallacies on the *Yes* side as you can. _____

_____

_____

_____

_____

_____

7. Briefly identify as many fallacies on the *No* side as you can. _____

_____

_____

_____

_____

8. All in all, which author impressed you as being the most empirical in presenting his or her thesis? Why? _____

_____

_____

_____

_____

_____

9. Are there any reasons to believe the writers are biased? If so, why do they have these biases? _____

_____

_____

_____

_____

_____

10. Which side *(Yes* or *No)* do you personally feel is most correct now that you have reviewed the material in these articles? Why?

_____

_____

_____

_____

_____

TAKING SIDES ANALYSIS REPORT (SHORT FORM)

Name: _____

Course: _____

Book: _____

Author: _____

Major thesis and position of author: _____

_____

_____

Answer the following as completely as you can from the material presented by the author:

1. Briefly state in your own words three facts presented.

_____

_____

_____

2. Briefly state in your own words three opinions given.

_____

_____

_____

3. Identify in your own words the propaganda techniques used, if any.

_____

_____

_____

4. What cause/effect relationships were stated or implied by the author?

_____

_____

_____

5. Were any of these cause/effect statements faulty? Why?

_____

_____

_____

6. Did you find evidence of other logical errors on the part of the author? Explain where and how for each of the topics listed below.

a. Distortion of Information _____

_____

b. Faulty Analogy _____

_____

c. Oversimplification _____

_____

d. Stereotyping _____

_____

e. Faulty Generalization _____

_____

7. How credible is the author? What are the author's credentials for writing this presentation?

_____

_____

_____

8. How does this material fit in with material in your text or material presented in class? Be specific.

_____

_____

_____

DECISION MATRIX

ISSUE: _____

NAME: _____

Taking Sides: _____

My Own ____

Position I:

_____

_____

_____

Position II:

_____

_____

_____

	AT BEST	AT WORST

SAMPLE DECISION MATRIX

Position I:

Violence on television causes aggressive behavior in children

Position II:

Violence on television does not cause aggressive behavior in children.

	AT BEST	AT WORST
	Children's aggressive behavior is minimized through parental monitoring of television viewing.	Children are permitted to watch anything they wish and, consequently, become highly aggressive.
	Children are free to happily watch anything they wish with no undesirable consequences.	Children do not learn to discriminate between valuable and trashy shows. Instead they spend lots of time watching television and become passive individuals.

ROLE-DESCRIPTION FOR INFORMAL DEBATES

All presentations should be brief, not exceeding 30 seconds. Say what needs to be said as concisely as possible. All members should help each other. Depending on the issue, some roles are easier to play than others. To make the 10-minute time limit, all should pitch in. It helps to take a few notes. This does not mean that statements need to be written out completely. Your statements should be informal and conversational.

Introducer — Is the leader and organizer of the group. The introducer's primary responsibility is to make sure progress is being made by each member on the objective. The introducer also states the point-counterpoint in general, using his or her own words, and gives a "lead-in" for the point-counterpoint by describing the topic in the text to which this particular issue is relevant.

Summarizer — Describes the specific point or counterpoint to which he or she has been assigned. The summarizer may give a brief statement on the background of the specific controversy and any other important information needed to understand the point-counterpoint.

Illustrator — Has the important responsibility of making the point-counterpoint relevant to the other students through examples, graphs, or in-class "experiments." How is the point-counterpoint important to the people in the class and what is a good way of illustrating the point?

Researcher — Reports any studies having some bearing on the particular side of the point-counterpoint to which he or she has been assigned. Some description of the research is appropriate, but mainly the studies' findings and conclusions should be presented. The researcher should also note important limitations or criticisms of the research.

Fielders — Answer any questions regarding the group's assigned point-counterpoint or the members' presentations. Fielders are also responsible for any important material omitted by a group member. Because fielders can be asked questions about members' presentations, it is a good idea to know what the other members are going to say.

PREPARING FOR A FORMAL DEBATE

Each issue will be debated by a panel of six students: three "pro" and three "con." Each team thus has three persons, each with a primary responsibility, as follows:

The *stater*. This person will be primarily responsible for stating the position taken by the group. He or she will bring up, point by point, the issues inherent in each part of the argument. A prepared written outline may be quite helpful, but direct reading of a prepared statement will not be appropriate. A conversational presentation of the position in the stater's own words will be much more acceptable. The stater will also be responsible for watching the flow of the arguments. At the end, the stater will summarize, recap, and state which of the points made can be salvaged to ultimately support the team's position.

The *prover*. The prover will be responsible for citing relevant research to back up any of the statements given by the stater. He or she must have intimate knowledge of the empirical content of the positions taken and should understand the research supporting the side chosen. The prover can do well by looking up outside sources in order to strengthen the stater's arguments. He or she can support points by using survey data gathered in class or outside. Any effort (short of murder) is legitimate for generating support for a position. However, the prover will be "attacked" at some length by the opposition—so he or she had better be able to back up his or her supporting data. It should be empirical and responsible.

The *attacker*. The attacker will be responsible for probing the opposite team for weaknesses in their arguments. He or she may question data, disprove, counter, and use any *rational* method to discredit the opposition's position or data. An appreciation for research design and data analysis may help the attacker. It is also strongly suggested that the attacker be very familiar with the articles and materials being used by the opposing team. Unless role-playing is extremely good, personal attacks are considered in poor taste. The questioner may insult one of the authors but should refrain from attacking the student who has that position.

A given debate might consist of the following points:

Pro—the pro stater makes his or her points.

Con—the con stater defines his or her counterpoints.

Pro—the pro prover brings on his or her evidence.

Con—the con prover delivers his or her data.

Pro—the pro attacker can move in.

Con—the con attacker can respond in kind.

Pro—the pro stater salvages all the undamaged arguments he or she has left and makes a summary.

Con—the con stater salvages all the intact arguments he or she has left and makes a concluding statement.

Other team formats are possible. For example, it would be feasible for the stater and the prover to work together, with each statement being supported by research as it is made. The questioners (pro and con) should restrain themselves until this procedure is over. Each team may layout its "attack" plan in advance. Members should stick as close to their formats as possible unless it becomes cumbersome when they are rebutted.

The *audience*. The students not involved in a debate are still a part of the situation. They will get special points for participation (and it will be noted by the professor). Two kinds of audience participation can be expected: clarification and question.

Clarification—If a student is uncertain of a point, counterpoint, interpretation of data, a study, or any other portion of a presentation, the students in the audience can ask for clarification. Whoever is explaining the concept or supporting members on the team should clear the problem up for the student as a teacher would do in any class. Clarification questions should be asked at any time (interruptions are fine).

Question—This kind of audience participation can come after a position is clarified and the research is in. Questioning is appropriate when a student is disturbed by an answer or has data to counter or expand upon a position taken by the panel. Please note that the panel (pro and con) is primarily responsible for this sort of question, and the audience should wait and see if the panel will develop the response before they question too deeply. Other kinds of audience participation and general discussion will be discouraged after the attackers have completed their jobs.

The *instructor*. You will know you are doing a good job if I [the professor] don't have to lead you by the nose to each point. I want *you* to do this work. There are no correct answers—no blacks and no whites. There are only mixtures of grays. The important point of this course is to find out how *you* view those gray areas.

DEBATE PREFERENCE SURVEY

ISSUE: _____

NAME: _____

BOOK: *Taking Sides: Clashing Views on Controversial Social Issues,* fourteenth edition

This survey is to find out which issues you might be most interested in discussing and how you feel about these issues. Your assignment is to read over the introductions of each of the issues by the next class meeting and fill out this survey and turn it in. No grade is given. Your preferences will be followed as closely as possible.

Issue	How much would you like to debate this topic? (check off choice)			Which side would you most like to have?	
	Very Much	**Some**	**Not at all**	**Yes**	**No**
1. Is American in Moral Decline?					
2. Does the News Media Have a Liberal Bias?					
3. Is Third World Immigration a Threat to America's Way of Life?					
4. Is the Decline of the Traditional Family a National Crisis?					
5. Should Mothers Stay Home with Their Children?					
6. Should Same-Sex Marriages Be Legally Recognized?					
7. Is Increasing Economic Inequality a Serious Problem?					
8. Is the Underclass the Major Threat to American Ideas?					
9. Has Affirmative Action Outlived Its Usefulness?					
10. Are Boys and Men Disadvantaged Relative to Girls and Women?					
11. Is Government Dominated by Big Business?					
12. Should Government Intervene in a Capitalist Economy?					
13. Has Welfare Reform Benefited the Poor?					
14. Is Competition the Reform That Will Fix Education?					
15. Should Biotechnology Be Used to Alter and Enhance Humans?					
16. Is Street Crime More Harmful Than White-Collar Crime?					
17. Should Drug Use Be Decrimianalized?					
18. Does the Threat of Terrorism Warrant Curtailment of Civil Liberties?					
19. Is Mankind Dangerously Harming the Environment?					
20. Is Globalization Good for Mankind?					

GUIDELINES AND FORMAT FOR THE SIMPLE DEBATE

INTRODUCTION

Each student will be responsible for presenting evidence to support one side of an issue regarding one of the major social institutions. The debate will be held during the week when the topic is under study in class. Depending upon the class size, each student will be responsible for a minimum of two and a maximum of four debates.

ORAL FORMAT

1. Each student will present an opening argument lasting a minimum of 5 and a maximum of 8 minutes.
2. Each student will rebut his or her opponent's argument in a maximum of 4 minutes.
3. Each student will present a second rebuttal and/or a final statement in a maximum of 3 minutes.
4. The entire debate should encompass 25 to 30 minutes.
5. Questions and comments from the class and instructor will conclude the debate.
6. No student will be permitted to read his or her speech. A written text may be referred to or an occasional quote may be read to the class. However, the student will present his or her arguments orally, in a coherent and logical fashion.

WRITTEN REQUIREMENTS

1. On the day a debate is to be given, be sure to hand in a typed outline with your major arguments listed. You may use this to help you present your arguments during the debate.
2. In your bibliography, list at least one outside source that presents an argument for your side of the debate and that is not contained in the assigned textbook.

GRADING

1. The written and oral debates will constitute 25 percent of the student's final grade.
2. Failure to inform the instructor beforehand and not showing up for the assigned debate will result in an F grade on that particular debate.
3. Grades will be based on an A+, A, B+, B, C+, C, D+, D, and F model. A+ = 95, A = 90, B+ = 85, B = 80, C+ = 75, C = 70, D+ = 65, D = 60, F = 55.
4. Grades will be based upon the clarity of the arguments, both written and oral. They will not be based upon a "winner" or "loser" in the debate. Upon occasion it might be worthwhile for a student to take the side of a debate issue with which he or she disagrees.

DEBATE EVALUATION FORM

Name: _____

Course: _____

Book: _____

COMPONENTS	POOR	FAIR	GOOD
ORAL			
INTRODUCTION	0	1	2
NEW INFORMATION	0	1	2
CONCLUSION	0	1	2
ORGANIZATION	0	1	2
ENTHUSIASM	0	1	2
WRITTEN (TYPESCRIPT)			
OUTLINE STRUCTURE	0	1	2
BIBLIOGRAPHY	0	1	2
SCHOLARLY SOURCES	0	1	2
PROOFREADING	0	1	2

GENERAL COMMENTS ON DEBATE PRESENTATION

STRENGTHS:

WEAKNESSES:

_____
Debate Score (18 points possible)
[Equivalent of a major test]

CLASS EVALUATION SCALE

NAME: _____

COURSE: _____

EVALUATION FOR: _____

For each question, use a scale of 0 to 4, with 0 = poor and 4 = excellent, to indicate your grade for each team (Pro and Con).

	PRO Team	CON Team
1. Did the team appear to have done its homework?		
2. Was the team presentation well organized and effective?		
3. Did the team make its presentation interesting to the class?		
4. Was the team empirical as it presented and defended its points?		
5. Did the team go beyond the issue as presented in the text?		
6. Was the team perceptive to the weak points on the opposite side?		
7. Did the team appear to work as a team?		
8. How effective was the stater?		
9. How effective was the prover?		
10. How effective was the attacker?		

INSTRUCTOR EVALUATION SCALE

STUDENT NAME:_____

DEBATE TEAM: _____

DEBATE TITLE: _____

For each question, use a scale of 0 to 4, with 0 = poor and 4 = excellent, to indicate your grade for each student.

	GRADE
1. Did the student appear to have done his/her homework?	
2. Was the student's participation in the debate well evident?	
3. Was the student's presentation well organized and effective?	
4. Did the student provide empirical evidence to support his/her arguments?	
5. Did the student make his/her presentation interesting to the class?	
6. Did the student make use of supporting materials outside of the readings?	
7. Did the student go well beyond the issue as presented in the text?	
8. Was the student perceptive to the weak points on the opposite side?	
9. Did the student appear to understand the key points on her/his side of the debate?	
10. Did the student anticipate well questions and/or opposing viewpoints?	

ISSUE EVALUATION FORM

Name: _____   Date: _____

Issue: _____

1. Before any current reading or reflection, I hold that:

_____

2. Based upon my reading of this controversial issue, I hold that:

_____

3. The major factors that lead me to this tentative conclusion are as follows:

a. _____

b. _____

QUESTIONS FOR PRESENTERS

YES: 1. _____

2. _____

NO: 1. _____

2. _____

Based upon my reading, listening, questioning, and reflecting on the material presented, I now/still conclude that:

_____

EVALUATION

My evaluation of the presentation is as follows:

YES Presenter _____   _____ NO Presenter
             _____ EXCELLENT _____
             _____   GOOD   _____
             _____   FAIR   _____
             _____   POOR   _____

Signature: _____

Appendices

APPENDIX 1

Sample Course Outline for Teaching with Taking Sides

This is a course outline that was prepared by Dr. Michael Reiner, associate professor of psychology at Kennesaw State College, Marietta, Georgia, for a course entitled "Psychology and Contemporary Issues." In addition to showing how Taking Sides can be utilized throughout a course, Dr. Reiner offers two approaches to controversy papers based on issues from the book.

Required Texts

Slife, B. (Ed.). (2005). *Taking sides: Psychological Issues* (14th ed.). Contemporary Learning Series, Dubuque, IA

Course Description

We are often confronted in the media, in our community, and in our personal life with problems that deal with psychological issues. The purpose of this course is to introduce you to a number of contemporary topics in order to illustrate how psychologists address these controversies. As is always the case in complex human affairs, there are no easy answers to many of the dilemmas we will investigate. Often, reality is not simply black or white, but is colored by an infinite number of subtle shades of gray. Therefore, when confronted by differing opinions and points of view, it is necessary to develop the ability to comprehend, evaluate, and make decisions in the face of uncertainty. The use of such "critical thinking skills" can have a profound impact upon one's life in terms of academic, professional, and personal success.

Course Objectives

1. To introduce you to a number of concepts, issues, and theories in contemporary psychology so that you will be a more intelligent consumer of information about psychology.
2. To provide you with thinking skills that will enable you to analyze, evaluate, and make decisions concerning complex contemporary issues in psychology.
3. To help you to improve your communications skills, both written and oral, in order to enhance your effectiveness in expressing your view on the issues. To this end, there will be many written assignments and much class discussion.

4. To encourage you to become more tolerant of ambiguity and diversity as it pertains to human experience and to increase your ability to deal with multiple points of view.

Course Requirements

1. **Attendance**—This class is discussion oriented. In order to learn, it is imperative that you attend class, read the material, and complete whatever homework is assigned *before* class. To reward those whose efforts to attend class show a commitment to the learning process, credit will be awarded based on attendance. You can earn up to *30 points* based on attendance.

   - 0–1 absences will get 30 points added to your TOTAL POINTS.
   - 2 absences will get 27 points added to your TOTAL POINTS.
   - 3 absences will get 24 points added to your TOTAL POINTS.
   - 4 absences will get 21 points added to your TOTAL POINTS.
   - 5 or more absences will get 0 points.

   Note: An absence on a day when a paper is due will count as *two* days absence.

   Of course, we all on occasion have times when we are ill or have a problem preventing us from attending class. You need not provide me with an explanation or reason for your absence because, in terms of learning from class, an absence is an absence regardless of the circumstances. *If absent from class, it is YOUR responsibility to find out what you missed. Being absent does NOT excuse you from anything that was discussed or due in class.* Make sure to find out what you missed *before* the next class. Also, all assignments must be turned in *on time* to receive full credit.

2. **Homework and Quizzes**—When we begin to address the issues in the *Taking Sides* book you will need to complete a homework assignment to prepare for an unannounced quiz on occasion. The quiz will be open note, thereby encouraging you to do the necessary homework. The purpose of the homework and quizzes is to help you to learn how to think critically about the material. This will facilitate your learning and should help

your grade on the papers and exam. There will be *EIGHT* quizzes/assignments on the twelve topics. Your grade will be based on your best *SIX*. Instructions on how to prepare for these classes will be provided at a later date. Each quiz assignment will be worth *10 points*.

3. **Participation**—Because this class is a seminar and not a lecture class, your active participation is required. Your participation will be evaluated, not on the quantity of what you say, but on the *quality* of your contribution to class discussion. I will provide you with feedback during the quarter as to my evaluation of your participation. Also, on occasion, I will ask you for a self-evaluation of your class participation to determine how things are going from your perspective. The midterm evaluation will be worth 50 *points*. The evaluation of participation for the remainder of the quarter will also be worth *50 points*.

4. **Ad Essay**—For the first class (The Media as Manipulator), you are to find an advertisement of interest in a magazine and answer the following two questions: 1) What are they trying to sell you? and 2) How are they trying to sell it to you? The purpose of this assignment is to try to "see below the surface" and critically analyze the way in which advertisers manipulate images and words to influence your behavior. You are to write an essay of approximately 250–300 words (about one typewritten page). The essay is due at the beginning of class and is worth 10 points.

5. **Controversy Papers**—At *TWO* points in the quarter, you will write more formal short papers pertaining to the reading and class discussion. At the beginning of classes termed "Controversy Paper" you will turn in a two-page paper based on *ONE* of the three preceding issues covered in class. In the paper, you will *discuss the evidence* on the issues based on the readings, *reach a conclusion* on the controversy, and *explain* the reasoning behind your conclusion. Your only sources will be the *Taking Sides* book, materials distributed in class, and class discussion. The *first* paper will be worth 50 points; the *second* paper will be worth *100* points. The papers will be *evaluated* in terms of:

Introduction
a) Grasp of the issue and points of view
b) Clear statement of your position based upon the evidence

Body of the Paper
c) A rationale provided to justify your point of view
d) Use of references to provide supporting arguments/evidence
e) Consideration of the opposing point of view and a rebuttal of the opposing arguments

Conclusion
f) Summary of your position and rationale; discussion of implications, applications, or ramifications

Style and Format
g) Accuracy of information, evidence, data

h) Clarity of writing (e.g., spelling, grammar, and form)
i) Proper citation and referencing of information

Papers are to be typed and double-spaced. DO NOT put your name on the paper. Only your *student number* ***(*or other identifying number—generally, social security numbers should not be required from students these days*) should appear to ensure objectivity in my evaluation. Late papers will be penalized by 10% because completed papers are essential for the discussion in class that day.

6. **Final Exam**—This will be an open-book, open-note essay exam. You will respond to questions based upon material from the readings and class discussions since the beginning of the semester. The purpose here is to see how well you can "think on your feet." The final exam is scheduled per the department. Make sure you check the time and place of the exam. There will be no exceptions, unless an emergency occurs. The exam is worth *100 points*.

Evaluation

Your *final grade* for the course will be calculated from the course requirements and will be weighted as follows:

Attendance (@ 30 points maximum)	30 pts.
6 Quizzes/Assignments (@ 10 points)	60 pts.
2 Participation Grades (@ 50 points)	100 pts.
Advertisement Essay (@ 10 points)	10 pts.
2 Controversial Issues papers (@ 50/100 points)	150 pts.
Final Exam (@ 100 points)	100 pts.
	TOTAL = 450 pts.

Your grades on assignments will be based upon the *quality* of your work. Your final grade will be determined by the TOTAL NUMBER OF POINTS you *earn*. The basis for letter grades is shown below:

A = at least 90% of 450 = 405 total points
B = at least 80% of 450 = 360 total points
C = at least 70% of 450 = 315 total points
D = at least 60% of 450 = 270 total points
F = less than 60% of 450 = 269 total points or less

Academic Honesty Policy

My interactions with you are based on the expectation of mutual trust and honor. You are required to do your own work on all class assignments, papers, and exams. Please do not give me any reason to be suspicious. If you violate this trust and are caught giving or receiving help on required assignments, you will be prosecuted as per the Kennesaw State College statement on Academic Honesty (see *Kennesaw State College Undergraduate Catalog*, with particular reference to "plagiarism" and "cheating"). Papers are to be the product of your own thinking and writing. Plagiarism of all forms is to be avoided at all cost. If you are in doubt as to whether some act constitutes a violation of the honesty policy, please ask me *before* it's too late!

How to Succeed in This Course: Suggestions from Former Students

At the end of last semester, I asked my class if they had any words of wisdom to pass on to the next generation (that's you!). Here is their advice to help you to succeed in this course:

- Stay current on all assignments. Do not allow yourself to get behind. Come to class regularly and pay attention. *Do* the homework assignments and come to class prepared!
- Read, do homework, participate in class discussions— It really helps.
- Get ready to write and have fun. Be thorough.
- Hang in there—you'll learn lots and have a lot of fun in the process.
- Be prepared to write a lot. (Homework and papers)
- Don't be concerned about the grade, try to understand the issues that are being discussed.
- Do your homework! The issue assignments will help you on your controversy papers and the exam. Do not miss class! You are responsible for material covered by videos shown in class, etc. If you miss, call someone and get specific details on what happened in class while you were absent. Some tests will ask questions regarding specific examples discussed in class. You will eventually get used to Dr. Reiner's New York accent! Enjoy.
- Remember that it is *evidence,* not opinion, you base your argument on. Don't let emotions cloud the issues.
- Do all your homework in the beginning so you can relax at the end of the quarter.
- Do read *all* the issues, and do all the homework, in order to better understand the issues.
- I would advise students to write down the pages on which they found the evidence while doing homework so that it would be easier to find when you take the final. (Don't just highlight in the book because it's harder to find that way.)
- Take Psychology 105 *only* with Dr. Reiner!

Please Note: In order to allow you to plan your life for the quarter, I try to remain on schedule. However, the class outline (see end of this appendix), as well as the above requirements and procedures, are subject to change in the event of unforeseen circumstances.

Controversy Paper #1

Below are questions pertaining to the "issues" examined over the past few weeks from the Taking Sides Psychological Issues text, 14th edition. Select ONE of the questions and write a two page "Controversy Paper." Instructions for writing the paper can be found [under] Course Requirement #5.

1. You are the director of the U.S. Department of Agriculture. There has been much heat on the department lately by animal rights advocates condemning the use of live animals in medical and psychological research that may cause pain and suffering. You must make a policy decision that will apply across the board, regardless of whether the research is invasive (such as vivisection) or not. Your policy must be "across the board" because it is impossible to know "where to draw the line." You have two options:

   a. You can *allow* research with *all* nonhuman animals.
   b. You can *prohibit* research with *all* nonhuman animals.

   Which do you choose? Why? Explain the rationale for your decision using the material from *Taking Sides* to support your argument (not your personal opinion on the issue).

2. You are a principal in a high school where a controversy has emerged with a student who has a difficult time paying attention to the material presented in class. The teacher explains to his parents that he should be seen by a physician and perhaps be given some medication to help him focus on the material at hand. His parents object on grounds that he has no physical or genetic problem, but that the school hasn't delivered the material in a way that would help their son understand it. You decide to call together the parents, the teacher, and a psychologist in attempting to provide the best situation for the student.

   What evidence would the psychologist provide for genetic behavior? What evidence would the parents provide for the concept of nurture rather than nature as an explanation for their son's behavior? Is there another concept that would better describe the rationale for the student's behavior? How would you resolve this issue to the benefit of the student? Explain the rationale for your decision using material from *Taking Sides* to support your position (which may or may not concur with your personal opinion on the issue).

3. The latest evidence is unclear as to the effect of divorce on the children of the marriage. Concerned as to the best way to deal with the situation that has placed their children in two different alternating homes and thus two different alternating schools, the parents have turned to a therapist to help them resolve this issue. What evidence can the therapist provide that divorce ultimately has no negative effect on the children and thus the parents should do what is their own best interest? What evidence can the therapist provide that divorce has many, both obvious and subtle effects on the development of the child? What advice would help the family determine the best method of handling the education and upbringing of their children? **Explain** the rationale for your decision using the material from *Taking Sides* to support your argument (not your personal opinion on the issue).

Controversy Paper #2

We have also examined the following three topics in this section of the course:

Issue #13—Is Drug Addiction a Choice?
Issue #15—Is Treating Homosexuality Unethical?
Issue #16—Do Video Games Lead to Violence?

For this paper, select *one* of the above questions. Write a paper that advocates the position that *opposes* your own.

For example, if you said "Yes" to issue #16, that indicates you believe that video games DO lead to violence. Now, write a paper arguing the case that video games do NOT lead to violence.

I am not concerned in this paper with your personal point of view. In fact, your paper will advocate a position *exactly opposite* your opinion on the matter. Therefore, based on the evidence, information, data, research, rationale, and arguments from *Taking Sides* and class discussion, defend the opposing position (i.e., the "underdog") from one of the above issues.

Please look at the directions for Controversy Papers in the syllabus ... When it mentions "your position," I am referring to the position you are *advocating* in the paper (not your personal opinion).

Please begin with a title. You may use the question itself from the Issue in the book, or be more creative. Make sure, though, that your title is informative (i.e., it tells the reader where you are going). The paper itself can be written as an essay answering the question or advocating a position. Alternatively, you may be more imaginative by creating a scenario, if you wish (e.g., as in Paper #1, arguing as the Director of the Department of Agriculture or the President of the United States).

In any case, make sure your stance on the question is clearly articulated. Make sure to present evidence and information from your sources to advocate your position. Provide documentation of your sources (if you refer to class discussion, cite the source as 'Reiner' in the paper; on the *Works Cited* page, specify 'Reiner, personal communication'). Do *not* present a *one-sided argument*. Make sure to acknowledge the alternative point of view and provide a critique of it.

Please Note: The assignment *requires* that you write a paper that advocates a view that opposes the one you specified earlier on the survey. Failure to do so will earn you no credit because you did not complete the assignment. If you have any questions about how to proceed, please feel free to ask me.

Think Hard! Write Well!

APPENDIX 2

Periodical Sources for Courses in American Government

The periodical sources discussed in this appendix have been prepared by Professor Larry Madaras of the Department of History, Howard Community College, Columbia, Maryland.

Students and instructors in search of more information for their debate subjects could consult the following sources:

1. *Annual Editions: American Government,* Bruce Stinebrickner, ed. (Contemporary Learning Series). Published annually since 1971, this volume contains over 50 carefully selected articles from some of the most important magazines, newspapers, and journals published today.
2. *Annual Editions: State and Local Government,* Bruce Stinebrickner, ed. (Contemporary Learning Series). Collection of over 60 selections from current periodicals that relate to the 50 state governments and approximately 80,000 local governments in the United States.
3. *Congressional Digest.* A monthly summary of timely issues.
4. *Congressional Quarterly.* A weekly report specifically on congressional activities.

Weekly magazines of various editorial persuasions may also be useful. Please note that most of these publications also have online versions. Some may need subscriptions. My [Professor Madaras's] assessment of the political orientation of the publications discussed here appears in parentheses.

1. *Human Events* (Conservative)
2. *The Nation* (Left-Liberal)
3. *The New Republic* (Liberal)
4. *Newsweek* (Liberal)
5. *Time* (Center)
6. *U.S. News & World Report* (Conservative)
7. *The Washington Post Weekly* (Liberal)
8. *The Washington Times Weekly* (Conservative)

Bimonthly magazines that examine issues and ideas relevant to the study of American government include the following:

1. *The Christian Century* (Liberal)
2. *Commonweal* (Left-Liberal)
3. *National Review* (Conservative)

Monthly magazines include:

1. *American Spectator* (Conservative)
2. *Commentary* (Conservative)
3. *The Progressive* (Left-Liberal)

Quarterly magazines include:

1. *Dissent* (Democratic Socialist)
2. *The American Prospect* (Left-Liberal)
3. *The National Interest* (Conservative)
4. *The Public Interest* (Conservative)

Newspapers are extremely useful, especially the Sunday summary of political happenings. See, for example:

1. The *Washington Post*
2. The *Baltimore Sun*
3. *New York Times*

APPENDIX 3

Leading Class Discussions of Controversial Issues

Prepared by Thomas E. Kelly

This is an article that originally appeared in the October 1989 volume of *Social Education;* it is reprinted here with permission. Thomas E. Kelly is an associate professor of education at John Carroll University, University Heights, Ohio. John Zola, whose "Scored Discussions" was a boxed insert in the original article, is a classroom teacher at Fairview High School and a clinical professor at the University of Colorado in Boulder, Colorado.

The evidence is ubiquitous. Whether we look at the colonists' decision to break with England, President Grant's treatment of the Nez Percé, the propriety of Iran-Contra affair, immigration policy, or mandatory drug searches in schools, it becomes clear that controversial issues permeate the social studies curriculum. In a pluralist democracy, we should expect nothing less. Addressing historical or current issues in the classroom can offer teachers and students a rich experience in democratic citizenship. The purpose of this paper is to propose constructive ways for discussing the issues.

The article deals with three matters: (1) a central goal with supporting rationale for social educators to consider when discussing controversial issues in the classroom, (2) selected discussion techniques that can contribute to this goal, and (3) whether teachers should disclose to students their personal positions on controversial issues.

The Goal: Informed, Reasoned Action[1]

Teachers in a democracy should conduct, not neglect, classroom discussions on curriculum-related controversial issues. They should do so to enhance the civic competence of students. A central attribute of this competence is the ability to engage in rational dialogue on complex public issues. To avoid genuine controversy in the classroom or to distort controversy to lead students to conclusions predetermined by the teacher to be correct is misguided for several reasons. Psychologically, avoiding genuine controversy may increase negative student attitudes toward social studies. Intellectually, avoiding or distorting controversial points of view is tantamount to an assault upon the intellect inasmuch as it denies students a rational assessment of the truth about a subject.

Morally, to suppress or distort competing perspectives is an affront to the dignity of students, treating them as means rather than ends and denying their standing as moral agents.[2] Such pedagogic stances, moreover, are counterproductive because they fail to achieve a durable allegiance. Students subsequently exposed to persuasive arguments previously withheld may respond with dogmatism, disillusionment, or defection.

To achieve psychologically rewarding, intellectually sound, and morally affirming positions on controversial issues, students need to engage in careful, reasoned assessment of the full range of relevant perspectives. Classroom teachers must ensure student exposure to a *best-case, fair hearing of competing points of view.* Such a procedural standard is met if the most articulate spokespersons for differing sides of an issue, had they been present for the full range of classroom discussion, would have judged that their points of view had been fairly and accurately represented in the discussion. The standard fails to be met if teachers regularly select the most articulate students to represent the preferred position in a debate; deliberately invite to class a representative of an alternative view whose personality or manner of presentation is likely to offend students and obscure the issues; use materials that are intentionally, even if not flagrantly, weighted for the desired position; selectively praise responses supporting the preferred position without paying close attention to the merits of the students' actual contributions.

This should in no way deny teachers their right to hold passionate substantive beliefs about particular controversial issues. As democratic educators, however, teachers should complement that substantive passion with a *procedural* passion that ensures a best-case, fair hearing for competing points of view. This procedural standard guarantees the expression of all positions, including the teacher's (see the final section for further remarks on this topic).

Conducting Discussions

There is no single formula for conducting good discussions. Yet a number of discussion strategies, when combined, may be effective. They are divided below into generic strategies and strategies that are germane to value controversies.

Generic approaches. There are at least six generic strategies germane to discussing controversial issues, whether factual, definitional, or valuational. These are (a) asking clear, focused questions,[3] (b) waiting for responses,[4] (c) calling on nonvolunteers as well as volunteers,[5] (d) promoting student-to-student interaction,[6] (e) probing for clarity, definition, and elaboration[7] and (f) checking to see whether one discussant understands another correctly.[8] These strategies can transform typical classroom discussion from a rapid, Ping-Pong encounter between the teacher on the one side and a few isolated, highly vocal students on the other to a sustained, thoughtful, and coherent conversation among a broad range of peers.

Values-related questioning strategies. One of the major sources of controversy involves conflicts in values. To promote a best-case, fair hearing, such controversies are perhaps best explained to students not as dichotomous conflicts between good and bad values but rather as disagreements in specific situations between properly weighting particular values that are generally attractive in some form to most people (e.g., equality, freedom, material well-being) or as dilemmas in which certain prima facie duties generally upheld (e.g., telling the truth, avoiding causing harm) conflict in particular situations.

Using the following six interrelated strategies, teachers can help students address controversial value issues thoughtfully.

1. Identifying the Central Value Conflicts
Judging which values should be upheld in specific situations presumes, at minimum, clearly recognizing the particular values in conflict. Teachers can facilitate this process by building a common vocabulary for describing values, possibly along lines proposed by Lockwood and Harris.[9] Explicitly identifying these values can set the stage for systematic and productive discussion.

2. Clarifying and Stipulating
One major source of public controversy is the ambiguity associated with predicting or controlling the actual consequences of policy decisions. A second is the difficulty of achieving consensus on the meaning of generally cherished values such as equality, justice, loyalty, and the common good. That is the case in part because definitions of these terms are prescriptive and value-based rather than descriptive in nature. Hence, probes to clarify meanings of terms used by students often serve to uncover implicit value positions. For example, how do you define 'loyalty' or 'justice'? In cases of disputed facts, predictions, or meanings of terms, stipulating can provide a sharpened focus on value issues. For example, if we say the effects will be ... or define loyalty as ..., how does that affect your view as to what is the right policy or action?

3. Comparative Justification
This kind of question extends general probes of students' reasoning and asks students explicitly to address the heart of the conflict: Why do they give greater importance to some values than to others in the case under discussion? For example, why in a specific case are property rights more important than governmental provision of a genuinely adequate minimum quality of material life?

4. Raising Comments to the Level of General Principle
These are probes that ask students to consider whether the particular priorities identified in one case should be generalized into a set of principles to guide actions in similar cases. For example, in the Anne Frank case, do students think it is always or ever right to lie to save a human life? Why? Posing analogous or slightly modified cases can help students test their tentative general principles. For example, if it were right to lie to save a relative's life, would it also be right to lie to save a friend, stranger, or enemy? If so, why? If not, what is the relevant moral difference?

5. Identifying Common and Uncommon Ground
Although the whole process of developing informed, reasoned positions on controversial issues is rooted in collaborative interaction, these probes particularly highlight that process. Teachers explicitly ask students to compare and contrast their views with those of others. For example, in what ways is your view similar to that of...? The common ground inquiry can be especially powerful for enhancing listening among adversaries who might otherwise tend to dismiss one another's views summarily.[10] Given such a relationship, the teacher can attempt with gentle insistence to engage students in expansive social role-taking, asking students to make conjectures about others' points of view, in the sense of generating sympathetically constructive reasons for holding those differing positions.[11] The point of this strategy is to nurture understanding, not necessarily consensus. Understanding through social role-taking is an essential part of developing an informed position and, as research indicates,[12] a necessary precondition to developing a fully reasoned moral position.

6. Comparing *Should* and *Would*
Ideally, we want students to only make informed and reasoned private judgments but, when appropriate, to act publicly in accordance with those judgments. In other words, teachers have a civic interest in whether students would act in particular situations as they think persons should act. In probing the relationship between *should* and *would,* teachers might be alert to students' concerns about incurring the charge of hypocrisy. If the personal level appears initially too threatening, teachers may ask questions at a generalized level. For example, are there factors that might interfere with persons' doing what they think should be done? How might a person deal with these factors constructively?

To Disclose or Not to Disclose

When conducting discussions on controversial issues, teachers are often asked to disclose their own positions.

Should they do so? Those who argue they should not cite several reasons. To do so might be politically imprudent inasmuch as teachers might be vulnerable to charges of coercive indoctrination from parents or students holding different points of view. In the current litigious climate, silence appears the safer and more appropriate strategy. It may also be wise to remain neutral or nondisclosing to sustain teacher authority, particularly in cases where teachers feel ambivalent about their own point of view. The claim is that students' respect for teachers diminishes if teachers' views appear confused or poorly conceived.

Turning from teachers to the best interests of students, teacher self-disclosure might be seen to undermine the central purpose of developing students' own critical intelligence on these controversial issues. This argument is particularly germane *for* students who are either highly impressionable or defiant or who believe that echoing the teachers' views is the easy or preferred route to good grades. From this perspective, teacher self-disclosure is seen at best as irrelevant and at worst as drawing students away *from* an objective assessment of the merits of competing perspectives.

Others would argue that teacher self-disclosure is potentially a positive act compatible with ensuring a best-case, fair hearing *for* competing perspectives. It is potentially positive *for* two key reasons. First, teacher self-disclosure with accompanying explanation can provide a constructive model to students on the complex and often hidden process of arriving at a reasoned point of view. In cases where teachers hold clear, though passionate beliefs, it can demonstrate that teachers are persons and citizens of conviction who give public witness to their values. In cases where teachers are ambivalent, sharing genuine struggle over the issues can provide validation and inspiration to students who may experience similar struggles. Second, authentic self-disclosure can minimize some of the distrust and resentment that occur when teachers conceal their personal point of view. Nondisclosure may be interpreted by students in various unfavorable ways—as a cowardly evasion of legitimate challenge to a teacher's point of view, as a presumptuous underestimation of students' independence of mind, as a frustrating denial of a potentially informative perspective, or as evidence of a fraudulent commitment to rational inquiry, or as an admission that certain views must be irrational or inferior if they cannot be articulated or defended reasonably.

When teachers reveal their own positions, they can minimize negative consequences by employing four practices: (1) publicly engaging in self-critique, (2) actively encouraging student critique of their positions, (3) sincerely praising reasoned competing viewpoints, and (4) honestly critiquing views that merely parrot those of the teacher. These practices are designed to place the evaluative emphasis where it belongs—on the merits and not the author or source of a particular position. Thus, although teachers possess greater power and authority in the classroom, they can and should direct these forces toward desirable ends; in our case, the end is the fundamentally civic one of informed and reasoned student positions on curriculum-relevant controversial issues.

Teachers should not be oblivious to political realities in schools nor should they insist upon sharing their unsolicited point of view on every controversial issue discussed. Strategic issues of timing, level of administrative support for the teacher, and student maturity, as well as the teacher's and community's particular positions on an issue, must all be considered judiciously. In the corrective context of a good-faith commitment to the standard of a best-case, fair hearing, teacher self-disclosure is a defensible and desirable posture to be embraced rather than avoided. Thus, where learners elect not to disclose, they should in general make clear their reasons for doing so. Attacks by parents on teachers' self-disclosure are essentially misguided attacks on democratic dialogue and suggest the need for educating parents, not preemptive self-censorship by teachers.[13]

Notes

1. The arguments in this and the last section draw heavily from an earlier paper. See T. E. Kelly, "Discussing Controversial Issues: Four Perspectives on the Teacher's Role," *Theory and Research in Social Education* 14, no. 2 (1986): 113–38. I use the term 'action' *for* two reasons: (1) to suggest that stating publicly one's position on a controversial issue is itself a form of social action and (2) to embed my work in the participatory strand of citizenship education that advocates active student involvement in the affairs of the multiple communities within which they live. See F. M. Newmann, *Education for Citizen Action: Challenges for Secondary Curriculum* (Berkeley: McCutchan, 1976); G. H. Wood, "A Voice for Progressive Change," in *Democracy and Education: The Magazine for Classroom Teachers* 1, no. 1 (1988), editorial preface.

2. J. Dewey, *Democracy and Education* (Toronto: Macmillan, 1944); M. A. Raywid, "The Discovery and Rejection of Indoctrination," *Educational Theory* 30, no. 1 (1980): 1–10.

3. R. Cruickshank, "Applying Research on Teacher Clarity," *Journal of Teacher Education* 36, no. 2 (1985): 44–48.

4. M. B. Rowe, "Wait Time: Slowing Down May Be a Way of Speeding *Up*," *Journal of Teacher Education* 37, no. 1 (January/February 1986): 43–50.

5. S. Kerman and M. Martin, *Teacher Expectations and Student Achievement: The Teacher's Manual* (Bloomington, Indiana: Phi Delta Kappa, 1980).

6. M. W. Berkowitz, "The Role of Peer Discussion in Moral Education," in *Moral Education: Theory and Application,* ed. M. W. Berkowitz and F. Oser (Hillsdale, New Jersey: Lawrence Erlbaum Associates, 1985).

7. A. Lockwood and D. Harris, *Reasoning with Democratic Values; Ethical Problems in United States History,* vols. 1 and 2, Instructors Manual (New York: Teachers College Press, 1985); F. M. Newmann and D. W. Oliver, *Clarifying Public Controversy: An Approach to Teaching Social Studies* (Boston: Little, Brown, 1970).

8. D. Harris, "A Curriculum Sequence *for* Moral Development," *Theory and Research in Social Education* 5, no. 3 (December 1977): 1–21.

9. Lockwood and Harris describe eight central values: authority, equality, liberty, life, loyalty, promise keeping, property, and truth (see teacher's manual, p. 4).

10. S. Berman, "Beyond Critical Thinking: Teaching *for* Synthesis," *Educators for Social Responsibility Forum* 6, no. 1 (Summer 1987): 1, 10.

11. M. F. Belenky et al., *Women's Ways of Knowing: The Development of Self, Voice, and Mind* (New York: Basic Books, 1986).

12. R. L. Selman, "Social-Cognitive Understanding: A Guide to Educational and Clinical Practice," in *Moral Development and Behavior: Theory Research and Social Issues,* ed. T. Lickona (Holt, Rinehart, & Winston, 1976), 299–316.

13. I wish to acknowledge Walter Parker's helpful editorial comments on an earlier draft of this paper.

Scored Discussions

Prepared by John Zola. The "scored discussion" strategy is one tool for helping students interact meaningfully with content and one another. In essence, the scored discussion is a fishbowl environment in which a small group of students carry on a content-related discussion while classmates listen. The content of the discussion is organized through use of discussion agenda. Monitoring the discussion process is the responsibility of students in the discussion group. Meanwhile, the teacher sits to the outside with the rest of the class and scores individual contributions to the discussion.

Students are awarded points for contributing relevant information, using evidence, asking clarifying questions, making analogies, and encouraging other group members to participate. Negative points are assigned for interruptions, irrelevant comments, and personal attacks. At the conclusion, the teacher and other students provide feedback on discussants' understanding of the content and of the discussion process.

Discussions can be as brief as 8–10 minutes, but 18–22 is recommended. Benefits include a clear structure for organizing study through use of the discussion agenda, opportunities to share knowledge aloud, an alternative means of evaluation, and positive peer interdependence.

The scored discussion strategy was first developed by Fred Newmann at the University of Wisconsin.

APPENDIX 4

Dialectical Thinking Matrix

This discussion was provided by professor Bart Macchiette from a longer article, "Debating the Issues: Adopting Critical Thinking in Contemporary Marketing Curricula"

Dialectical thinking involves the understanding and resolution of refutations—looking for, recognizing, and welcoming contradictions as a stimulus to development, which is central to argumentation and debate. It presumes change rather than a static notion of reality, and truth is always emergent, never fixed; relative not absolute (Daloz 1986). *Dialectical thinking* in debates can be enhanced by encouraging students to look at all points of view and discussing and evaluating the merits of each case or scenario. While in most cases, students are required to consider the debate as a black or white issue by taking either a pro or con stance, Slife and Rubenstein suggest a Decision Matrix (Slife 1994) format that forces students to consider all possible scenarios to a complex issue. They are asked to speculate both the best as well as the worst case scenarios that might follow from adopting either position in the debate. A modified form of such a matrix is presented below, which illustrates how a student can be encouraged to take a 360-degree view on an issue such as, for example, whether or not outsourcing is good for the U.S. market. The matrix enables students to broaden the horizons by identifying and challenging the assumptions, considering the importance of context, and imagining and exploring alternatives and seeing the debate from various perspectives.

Figure 1

Sample Decision Matrix Tools to Frame a Debate Enhancing Dialectical Thinking

	ALTERNATIVE SCENARIOS	
	BEST CASE	WORST CASE
PRO Position: Outsourcing is Good for the U.S. Market	Outsourcing creates robust and efficient global and U.S. markets, greater innovation and lower prices.	Outsourcing creates global competitiveness and challenges U.S. businesses to keep up with the rest of the world.
CON Position: Outsourcing is Bad for the U.S. Market	Outsourcing causes only temporary loss of jobs in the U.S., most of which are replaced by better jobs in the long run.	Outsourcing results in permanent loss of jobs in the U.S. and is detrimental to its economy in the long run.

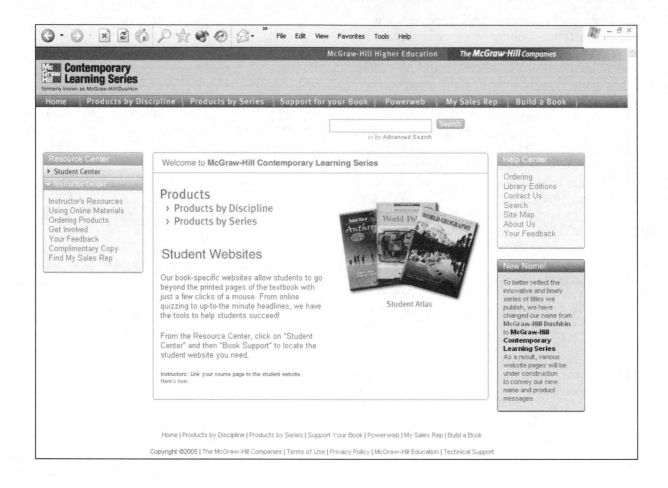

Learn more . . .

Visit our website and browse through our complete list of current titles.

With **McGraw-Hill Contemporary Learning Series**, you can easily incorporate current issues into your course. These inexpensive readers will help your students develop critical thinking skills and inspire serious dialog in the classroom.

SHARE YOUR SUCCESSFUL INSTRUCTIONAL METHODS

If you've developed an interesting or unique way to use *Taking Sides* in your classroom, we would like to hear about it! It might be simple—a game, a discussion method, a special technique to generate student interest, a testing procedure—or it might be an entire unit built around an *Taking Sides*. Either way, we hope you'll share it with us. Please photo copy this page, briefly describe your idea—preparation, materials needed, instructions to students, etc. If possible, include copies of the printed instructional materials you used to implement your idea or strategy. If we use any of your materials, you'll receive full credit in print.

Dear McGraw-Hill Contemporary Learning Series:
Here's what I did using (book title) *Taking Sides:* _____(add an extra sheet, if needed):

_____
_____
_____
_____
_____
_____
_____
_____
_____
_____
_____
_____
_____
_____
_____
_____
_____
_____
_____
_____
_____

Name _____ Date: _____
School: _____
Department: _____
Address: _____
        Street and Number   City   State   ZIP
Office telephone number or e-mail address (in case we need more information or clarification):
(_____) _____ _____
Area Code   Number   E-mail address:

Mail to: McGraw-Hill Contemporary Learning Series
                 2460 Kerper Boulevard
                 Dubuque, IA 52001-9902

Or you can access this form to interact directly with us on our online Web site:
http://www.mhcls.com/online/contentsmain.mhtml